GOING DRY

MY PATH TO OVERCOMING HABITUAL DRINKING

SEAN ROBINSON

Copyright © 2022 Sean Robinson

All rights reserved. No portion of this book may be reproduced, stored in a retrieval system, or transmitted in any form or by any means—electronic, mechanical, photocopy, recording, scanning, or otherwise—except for brief quotations in critical reviews, articles, or groups, without written permission of the author/publisher at www.seanrobinson.ca.

Going Dry: My Path to Overcoming Habitual Drinking
Robinson, Sean
ISBN 978-1-7781817-1-9 (Paperback)
ISBN 978-1-7781817-0-2 (e-book)
ISBN 978-1-7781817-3 3 (Paperback IS)
ISBN 978-1-7781817-2-6 (Hardcover)

Co-Edited by Katie Beaton of Veneration
And Christine Bode of Bodacious Copy
Cover art by Ruud de Peijper.
Book production and cover design by
Dawn James, Publish and Promote.
Interior layout and design by Perseus Design.

Printed and bound in Canada.

Note to the reader: The events in this book are based on the author's memories from his perspective. The information is provided for educational and inspirational purposes only.

Dedicated to my wife, Angela, and our children, Liam, Nash, and Ellie. For you, I chose to be better. For you, I will do the work to stay better. And for me, I will enjoy every minute of it.

In appreciation for every podcast, book, and conversation that helped motivate me to make the change I needed and for everyone that may find inspiration from my experience.

CONTENTS

Introduction 7
CHAPTER 1: New Year's Resolutions 11
CHAPTER 2: Habits and Routines 21
CHAPTER 3: Cottage Season. .33
CHAPTER 4: Childhood Lessons. 41
CHAPTER 5: Pass the Ice 51
CHAPTER 6: Celebration Time. 57
CHAPTER 7: The Test. 63
CHAPTER 8: Turning the Corner. 75
CHAPTER 9: The Wedding 87
CHAPTER 10: No Umbrellas. .95
CHAPTER 11: Year's End. 103
CHAPTER 12: It's Your Turn, Challenge Yourself . . . 113
About the Author. 119

INTRODUCTION

FLASHBACK
Journal entries, summer of 2020:

I don't know what to do. Where do I even begin? It appears that I am a journal person now. What have I become? A man doesn't keep a journal, a man doesn't show emotion, and a man never shows weakness. I am having such a hard time getting myself straight. I feel so happy and so lost all at the same time. I have the hardest time with my weight, my motivation is awful, and my family is missing me. I need to be a better person. I know what I need to do, so why can't I do it? WHAT IS WRONG WITH ME!? Why can't I be the man my wife deserves and the father my kids will be proud of? I am better than this.

What am I going to do with this journal? What if someone finds out that I am writing about my problems? How will I explain this? I really hope this helps me. I don't know what to do. I have the hardest time getting out of bed in the morning. I will do whatever I can to keep my work volume down, and I will find excuses not to play with my kids or do things with my family *because I am tired or because I don't have the drive. This can't be how I live my life. Stop being so negative and stop making excuses. Get your shit together!*

COVID-19. A global virus that shut down countries around the world in 2020. We all dealt with it in our own ways. The full closures and lockdowns set me up in a bad way early on, mainly because, like most, I was neither mentally nor physically prepared for what the next couple of years would bring. When the first lockdowns started, I was working on my latest version of the eat less and move more lifestyle. I was dieting and exercising more, losing weight and feeling good. When this shutdown happened, nothing like it had ever happened to us or any of the eldest people in our families. We didn't know how to deal with it, and we couldn't believe we were told to stay at home and that things were shut down.

Not being able to go anywhere or do anything made it easier for me to leave my newest health kick behind. I didn't yet know how to work around something this drastic with my routine. I took a break while in lockdown (I couldn't have gone to the gym even if I wanted to) and found new ways to live my life. My lifestyle and social circle already included heavy drinking. Being stuck at home made things worse. I thought *I could have a few drinks if I can't go anywhere or do anything*. That was the start of a bad year for me. I had such a good start, but very quickly, I found that my progress was not sustainable in such a life-altering situation. I was barely in the groove with my diet and fitness regime. There was no way I was ready for a complete shutdown. In the

INTRODUCTION

beginning, it felt innocent and harmless. While some non-essential stores were temporarily shut down to stop the spread of COVID-19, there were never huge restrictions on liquor stores and beer stores. It became customary to drink each night while on Zoom parties with friends, stuck at home with no other plans. I got creative by mixing the new popular flavoured vodka with other flavoured vodka drinks like a true drinking champion. That summer was not my proudest moment. I'm not sure what I was trying to prove. I was having some rough nights and rougher mornings. My family deserved a better version of me.

In no time, we were closing on the first year of our new normal in Ontario, Canada. I was heavier than I had been when I had started the previous year. I was thinking, *why am I such a failure? Why can't I figure this out and stay focused?* Things like this and many more self-harming words were written in my journal. I have *never* been a journal guy and had only written a few things, but it was not a feel-good place for me. I needed to get these thoughts out of my mind. I needed to see them written and then buried in a place where only I knew where to find them. I didn't know what to do or how to fix it; I was sure that drinking each night and the tension it created for me with my then pregnant wife, Angela, and our two young boys was not good for any of us. I would never wish harm on myself or wish that I wasn't on this Earth, but I was not nice to myself. I needed something to change. Yet I also didn't feel like I had a problem with drinking. I just thought that I was having a good time and that this is what everyone must have been doing. That is normal, isn't it?

Alcoholism is a serious subject, and it has affected many lives. It can be through someone's drinking or the drinking of a close friend or family member. In no way do I promote or encourage irresponsible drinking. Instead, I encourage everyone to check themselves now and then to ensure they aren't hurting themselves and those around them. It can be subtle. You may not realize that it is as obvious and harmful to those around you as it is.

I do not intend to judge anyone or any situation involving drinking alcohol with this book. It is merely a glimpse into my case and experiences. At the time of this writing, I have been fortunate not to have had a serious life-changing incident involving alcohol. I maintain that I have led a responsible "party" life. Not everyone can relate to a traumatic episode involving alcohol, which is not always a benchmark for change. However, we can work on improving our lives and create positive routines to come out of discomfort and displeasure, not just a place of trauma and pain. Whatever your reason, and whatever your background, you can change. You can create a better routine. You can control your drinking and your life.

I am thirty-seven years old, a father of three kids under age nine, a husband, a construction worker, and a volunteer firefighter. The expectation to drink follows me everywhere. Yet, I needed to take a break from drinking for myself and everyone else in my life. That is how I started 2021.

CHAPTER 1

NEW YEAR'S RESOLUTIONS

January 1, 2021—the beginning of the year. The freshest of starts to be had by all. The first day of my newest resolutions. Well, maybe not the first day. *I feel awful today; I am going to start tomorrow. But tomorrow is a Saturday, so how about I start on January 3? That would be a Monday, and Mondays are so much easier to start new things or give up old ones.* Really? Start something on a Monday?

It's Monday . . .

I always seemed to postpone changing all the things that bothered me about myself (how I felt, how my last year went, how much money I had in the bank, etc.) to the very last day of the year and well into the following year, if I got to them at all. It always seemed like a lot of work to change. So much buildup. *This year, I will be different!* Please. I was just another person with a fresh gym membership in January with about a month's worth of drive and another six months of wasted payments before I cancelled, again. I did this to myself every year. I used the magic of January to help push me to make resolutions to change. I stopped calling them resolutions because, secretly, I was upset at myself for never following through. It seemed like it wasn't so bad to fail on what I had set up for myself if it wasn't my resolution. If it was simply something I wanted to work on this year. It wasn't so bad if I gave up and jumped off the wagon.

A few things were happening in my life leading up to that January moment that I wasn't proud of. There were a few stories in the years prior that I wish had a different outcome and quite a few mornings of misery and pain that were certainly avoidable. What things in my life did I want to "work on" this year? (I downgraded the importance of a resolution to help myself when I failed.) I could have tried losing weight, eating better, taking courses, saving money, spending more time with my family, and strengthening my relationships with my wife, kids, parents, and friends. Basically, the same things I picked from every year. *This January thing just isn't fun for me. Why do I do this to myself if I am not going to change? Is there something I don't see, something else I can work on?*

In the few years leading up to this, I had developed quite a routine, whether I knew it consciously or not. I kept a well-stocked fridge in the garage, where I spent most of my time. In the basement fridge, there was an equally stocked bar. I had only lived in that house for a couple of years by this time, but it didn't seem to matter where I lived as it was just something I'd always done. I kept the bar and fridges stocked, not only because my obsessive-compulsive tendencies and previous bar/restaurant employment experience told me to, but also because you never really know when a party or get-together might break out or if I was going to feel like having ten to twelve beers after work. The strange thing about this routine was that I didn't always have to do the same thing to feel like drinking. I could be barbecuing, cutting the grass, watching the game, watching a movie, having a meal (usually not breakfast; after all, I didn't feel like I had a problem), at a restaurant, building/fixing something, talking to a friend, etc. It didn't matter what I was doing. Somehow, it felt like I should have something alcoholic on the go, and why stop at one? I didn't bring alcohol with me to work, and I never drank while driving or operating equipment. But if I was set up for the day/night or had arranged a ride home, it was "go time."

Go time. Here is where my routine became problematic for me. Somehow, somewhere along the way, I got it into my head that the only way I would maximize the situation was to drink these mandatory and delicious beverages as quickly and as consistently as possible to get that buzz faster, let loose and have a good time. The problem with this is that this pace was the same pace I would maintain all day/night. It wasn't just a race to get to a buzz because I couldn't turn it off. I felt like I had to drink everything I brought with me (which was usually more than I needed) or keep pace until bedtime from my stocked fridges. That wasn't a daily event. I didn't feel like I needed it every day, and there were even weeks sometimes that I didn't have anything. But, if it was a party, wedding, Friday or Monday, and people were drinking, it would be no problem for me to have a few drinks or more. Insert a pandemic here with stay-at-home orders in effect.

According to Google and the Oxford Languages Dictionary, the definition of a problem is "A matter or situation regarded as unwelcome or harmful and needing to be dealt with and overcome." *Wow, that is specific. I don't have a problem. Sure, I have a few too many, and I can be a bit abrasive, but a problem? I'll just take it easy next time; I won't have as many. I don't have a problem. I haven't had anything to drink in like a week. I didn't sleep much last night and barely ate, that's why.* These were all things that I had thought of when reflecting on the day before. It is tough to associate casual drinking with an alcohol problem. Many associate having an alcohol problem with a traumatic event, a relationship breakdown, and/or legal issues. These are extremes, but only you can determine if your drinking is problematic.

And that is what I did leading up to my passive January 1-ish starting point. At the time, I didn't know about stopping altogether that year, but I was going to have a Dry January.

Dry January. I had heard of people doing this before. It seemed the whole year would fly by, and we'd go from drinking on weekends to during the hockey game to while camping or at the beach to on long weekends and birthdays to Christmas and New Year's parties. Now, I was going to take a break from drinking, and I was going to make it to February without alcohol.

NEW YEAR'S RESOLUTIONS

My main problem with even considering this as an option was that I didn't have any reason to think this was possible. To feel better about me, repair any broken relationship, or work on becoming more focused and healthier by not drinking was probably the last thing on my mind. Nobody in my circle of close friends and family was spending a portion of their life sober. Some I had interacted with would be sober and not drinking, but those people always seemed older than me and had their own stories for why they weren't drinking. Those stories were often unknown to me and awkward just the same. No matter their reasons, it was out of respect for them and the room I was in not to pry. If it was from trauma, I didn't want to be the reason someone brought it up. Many times in my life, I have found my foot in my mouth for speaking, and you could say I had learned my lesson.

Another reason this was not something I considered was that I didn't have a clear memory of not having a drink. I will get to some of my early influences later. But with so much drinking around me as a child, it was like a rite of passage to drink. A couple of years before I was of legal drinking age, my friends and I would have field parties and house parties (adults were often nowhere around). And nights when our fake IDs would get us into the bar. That was a risky time, and the rush of being able to play like the adults played was a good feeling. When you are seventeen and know everything, it only makes sense to be allowed to drink, right? The rite of passage would come when we could legally drink, and we would celebrate. Our parents, relatives, and friends rushed to buy us our first drinks and legally bought them whenever we wanted to (whether it made financial sense or not). When you know almost everyone at the bar on any given Thursday, Friday, Saturday, and Sunday night, it is like a celebration every weekend. This time of my life and the happiness surrounding me followed me into my twenties.

As I reflect now, I know there was a point when I felt like I was chasing not only the buzz that I had at nineteen years old but also that version of me and my experiences at that time. The problem, which I will get into more later, was that this is where my biggest concerns were. I was not going to find this person. While chasing him down to the bottom of every bottle, can and case, he made me feel more distant, irritable, and unsure. My immediate memory of drinking and getting to that buzzed state—and never finding it the same way I thought I remembered it—set me up for a very unhealthy routine and expectation around drinking.

I finished off my "last drink" of the year on January 4. I remember this because I crushed the can in my fist, wrote the date on it with a sharpie, and put it on the shelf above my bench in the garage, where I often saw it. I wrote every bit of this book in the garage, where I feel the most at home, while the crushed can stared at me over the computer screen. I didn't know then, but if I were successful, I would remember when my last drink was. I would be able to count the days and become increasingly prouder that I could handle taking an entire month off. If I weren't successful, I would just add this graffitied can to the bag and get my ten-cent deposit back when I restocked my supply.

I wasn't ready to call it a resolution, but something felt different. It was way too early to tell, but maybe I wanted something to change this time. I felt like I had to relearn how to do things. How was I going to barbecue without a drink? How was I going to watch the big game without a drink? How was I going to do anything without a drink? Ever since I was of legal age, I had never gone more than a few weeks without a drop of alcohol. So before getting too excited, I guessed I should figure out what my ground rules would be.

Rule 1: No pretending. I didn't want to run to the 0 percent or 0.5 percent options. I know people have been drinking these for years and that even the big companies are spending more money and effort to provide them. But I wanted my entire routine to change. I wanted the mechanism of drinking and the habit I had to change. How was I going to do that while still pretending?

Rule 2: Fit in. There is such an awkwardness to being the only one in the room not drinking. I would learn much more about this soon enough. In the beginning, I especially didn't want the attention. So I needed to figure out how I would fit in while not "playing the game." I bought a decent drinking cup. The plan was to buy one, and this would be what I used when I was "drinking." I would bring a few other drink options to pour into my new cup, a few things that I could drink. I'd have regular conversations or continue with the day-to-day tasks that I didn't think I could do before without a cold beer. I would stand there, holding my cup, drinking my non-alcoholic option, having a good time, and nobody would be the wiser.

Rule 3: Stay the course. Those next thirty days sober was going to happen, and I was committed to it. I never intended to rush back into it at the end of thirty days. I took it one day, one visit, and one event at a time. I'd politely turn down any offers, shrugging it off as a Dry January because everyone understood and everything was good. I could do this.

That was uncharted territory for me. Never had I purposely avoided alcohol in such a way. I had never felt like I needed to. Establishing rules, what was I doing? Three seemed like plenty. What else was there? Don't fake it; fit in and keep going.

As January continued, people around me started to drop off with their commitment to a Dry January. We never determined that we were doing this together. It was my goal, and it just so happened that I had family and friends working on their version of it. I couldn't let others make me think that I shouldn't continue, that two weeks was enough and that I should be proud that I had made it that far. I didn't make anything; I was only halfway there. With others also not drinking and my rules in play, January flew by, and I started to be OK without drinking.

February is here. I made it. I was feeling better already, enjoying my mornings with my family. With my three young kids, the days start early. It was nice not waking up and being miserable, hungover and unavailable to help. I think my wife was beginning to like this new person I was becoming. *Maybe I will do another thirty days. February is a short month anyway; it won't be so bad.* The Canadian Cancer Society promotes Dry February. Some people choose between one or the other. I don't often hear of too many people doing both months. In fact, I only ever hear of people doing a couple of weeks during these two months and calling it a win.

I am not judging. Who am I to determine what kind of break someone else needs, what their drinking was doing to them, or their reasons for change? In the beginning, people couldn't believe I was still not drinking, and they would laugh off their weak attempts at taking a break. They couldn't make it more than a given term because of an event, someone's birthday, or a Friday.

Midway through February, I worked an hour away from home and needed a break from the radio on my drives. I love music, but two hours a day of the same songs? I needed something else. I have always been a fan of different genres and have streaming accounts like Spotify that I use often. But I thought there might be a better use of my time on the road than listening to the same songs and depressing news every day. I had never been a talk radio guy, and the thought of listening to podcasts or books was NEVER something I was into. Where would I even start? It could be the impression left on me from growing up, my friends, or my cultivated views, but podcasts and audiobooks were for "those people." I have no idea who "those people" might be, but I didn't feel I was the self-help kind of guy who listens to interviews of people talking about how they have solved the world's problems in their new book. These were never resources that I thought would work for me. To me, they always seemed so weak and so vulnerable.

Men needed to be strong. Men needed to listen to loud music and drink lots of beer. To be different from this would bring ridicule and pressure (bullying, if you will) from friends and family who didn't understand. So far, I wasn't ready to talk to many people about not drinking. I definitely wasn't going to talk about podcasts and books either. But, as I researched what content was available and how it might fill my driving time, I started to feel like this would be very good for me. Maybe "those people" had something figured out that the rest of us should know.

I found a few podcast programs with inspirational content and quickly found myself in a wormhole of information on many different topics. For example, I discovered so much inspiration and encouragement from *The Model Health Show* with Shawn Stevenson, the *School of Greatness* with Lewis Howes, and *The Ed Mylett Show*. And so, I started to develop different goals and ideas for improving myself in more ways than not drinking. As I listened each day and looked forward to my drive to and from work, I had my eyes on the end of February. I was going to get through my second month alcohol-free.

CHAPTER 2

HABITS AND ROUTINES

It is interesting to take a break from the pace of life to realize that we don't know everything. We know enough to get by, enough to keep ourselves alive. Ultimately, we know enough to be dangerous. The stigma about not asking for help and not appearing weak has followed me my whole life. I don't know where this came from, but this mentality meant self-help and inspirational content were for someone else. It was for people with problems. I thought I didn't have problems; I was normal. But it seems the more you learn, the more you realize you don't know. The more you understand, the more you realize we are all the same. We are human, and we all have similar things to enhance.

In such a short time, I could pick and choose as I looked through years and years of experience and conversations available from each of the people I mentioned earlier. These men discussed topics I wanted to learn more about in these programs. Some of the biggest celebrity influencers, such as Kobe Bryant, Terry Crews, and Matthew McConaughey, covered such topics. These were all people whom I had enjoyed watching compete or perform, yet I never thought they had so much happening behind the scenes. Looking for people I felt I could relate to, mainly through knowing who they were, helped as I started.

I looked forward to my drives to work and back every day. I would also listen while shovelling the driveway or walking on the treadmill at home. At first, I felt like the interviews I heard were for the guest to promote their books and personal podcasts. Still, as I got over myself and stepped down from my pedestal, I felt very different. As I opened to giving the podcasts a chance, I created an Audible account and purchased my first audiobook.

Mel Robbins is such a good speaker. I was impressed with her interview and her story promoting her book, *The 5 Second Rule: Transform Your Life, Work and Confidence with Everyday Courage.* She hooked me after hearing her no-shit attitude and description of her worst moments, which led to her coming up with *The 5 Second Rule* and writing the book. I purchased this book on Audible, and Mel read it to me and told me everything I needed to hear. In a moment where I needed something that would pick me up when I didn't have the drive, a version of this rule helped immensely. I found myself counting down from three (five was way too much as I felt silly and would convince myself otherwise), and then I would act. It may not have been that I jumped up and ran a marathon, but I would get up and make a move, any move helping me progress forward. Exactly what the

HABITS AND ROUTINES

rule was trying to do. As I listened to it more and more, it gave me some tools I could use, some reassurance to make me feel like I was making the right move and a way to feel better about the path I had chosen. So much I was feeling and journaling about at the beginning of the year was already coming to light. One month without drinking had given me so much already.

Having completed a month without alcohol and beginning to listen to some fascinating people talk about their experiences, I was learning a lot about habits and routines. We have all programmed ourselves to follow our habits and routines automatically. We do them in response to another action and without much thought. Some practices include turning the light on when you enter a dark room, putting your shoes on before walking outside, and covering your mouth when you sneeze. We are programmed to do many things when we feel a certain way or respond to another action.

Some of my patterns around drinking were as simple as grabbing a beer because I was home from work as everyone drinks when they get home. Another is when the game is on. Literally, every other ad is about the coldest, most refreshing alcoholic beverage. So, I had many habits around drinking in a whole variety of different situations and environments.

While working on determining my triggers, it was interesting to be conscious of the different times I craved alcohol. My peers and social expectations told me I needed to be always ready to drink. Still, it was important for me to know for sure when I was craving a drink so that I learned how to manage that craving differently. It was interesting to find out that I really didn't feel thirsty; it was just easy to go to the fridge and open another bottle or can. Like when we are bored, we go for a snack whether we are hungry or not. Some ideas were so simple that it was surprising I didn't know them already. It was interesting to learn about routine, the process of learning a new habit or stopping an old one, and the different theories about the number of days it takes to complete this.

I am sure we have all heard that it takes twenty-one days to break a habit. Some argue that this twenty-one-day period is a cycle, so maybe you need more than one cycle to change yourself. Others are firm that breaking a habit takes sixty days. One even said that one hundred days would change your life. One hundred days—I don't think I have ever knowingly done anything for one hundred days in a row. That stayed in the back of my mind as I listened to more and more podcasts of people talking about their experiences, books, education, and passions. Another stressed the importance of keeping track of your goals and progress in a journal or on the calendar. *Journaling, I don't think so,* I thought. *That's not me. I would never write my thoughts and experiences down for someone else. That kind of vulnerability is not who I have become, not something I'll ever be capable of.* But the calendar idea was intriguing. I could mark the calendar every day I completed a task and do it without anyone that saw it knowing what it was. No exposure meant no vulnerability.

I started marking the calendar. I wasn't sure yet about continuing for one hundred days. Still, it was nice to follow the circled numbers as my mini victories, each day successfully passing without so much as a sip of alcohol. By the second week of February, I felt very comfortable with my system, and it felt good to still work on my goals for the new year. The closer it got to the end of February, the more one hundred days was clearer to me. So that was my new goal. I was going to keep doing this, and I was going to get to one hundred days. In the beginning, thirty days had seemed nearly impossible, but with my system in place and my rules working for me, one hundred days was the new thirty.

I even started working on a few other goals I intended to continue implementing—things from brushing my teeth twice a day to exercising more and reading. My calendar had so many different circles, boxes, notches and notes, each for another item. At the beginning and end of each month, I wrote where I was for each goal, so I didn't lose track. I felt good and less irritable because I was winning at this year's resolutions. Whether I was calling them by name or not, they were still resolutions.

As I got closer to day fifty, the halfway mark of my new goal, all the people around me taking a similar alcohol-free break had returned to their previous ways. The conversations changed.

"You STILL aren't drinking?"

"Wow. One hundred days, what for?"

"So, you are quitting?"

"No alcohol at all, not even Baileys in your coffee?"

I love coffee, and on the weekend, especially in the winter, a little Baileys or similar cream liqueur in my coffee was the hardest thing to surrender. I even made sure to buy the latest seasonal flavours so I wouldn't miss out on them for a time when I would drink and enjoy them again.

As the conversations changed, I started to feel more judgment come in my direction. It was amazing how people could not comprehend how someone would decide to take one hundred days off drinking. There was such an awkwardness about it that my response simply emphasized that I wasn't quitting, just taking a break. Whenever it came up with friends, family, and co-workers, I felt I had to defend my decision.

On more than one occasion, my brother commented, "Well, did you get your coin yet? Are you ready for a beer?"

While he playfully joked, I was too anxious about all of this to brush this comment off. Although I wanted to tell him where to go, I bottled this up, as I did with most other remarks and stored it away. This reaction from people just pushed me to keep going. Ultimately, it was nobody else's business that I wasn't drinking. I felt that people just didn't know how serious I was about it. I wasn't that open to those around me. It must have been confusing for them to try and understand.

At the start of the year, committing to a Dry January was much harder with the pandemic restrictions. The pandemic had allowed, banned, and reallowed group gatherings while encouraging social distancing. Even with things starting to open and social circles broadening, avoiding functions and maintaining distance was more acceptable. It was next to impossible to get certain parts and pieces for things at other stores. However, I could confidently (in my mask and with sanitized hands) go to the liquor or beer store and load up for a time when I wasn't going anywhere after work. I could drink with my friends over Zoom or Teams all night. In contrast, when I began my resolution, the limited social gatherings and encouraging distance also helped me by creating fewer social functions where drinking was involved.

The longer I stayed dry, the more difficult Rule 2—to fit in—became. I was OK with people knowing now, as I was proud of myself for every day that passed. It was much easier that people knew, but it didn't take a certain awkwardness away. Each time I was in a drinking environment, remembering that I would be drinking in the past, it surprised people that I was drinking water, even if I tried to hide my drink of choice in my fancy "drinking" cup. There were the same conversations about quitting, inevitable digs about being "that guy," and playful jokes at my expense—as if the only way to be included at a party was to be on the same level as everyone else. Nobody wants that sober guy around who will remember everything and not feel awful the next day. I know this because I heard this from friends in a couple of different circles.

It was supposed to be harmless, but there was an element of self-consciousness to my mission that didn't need this kind of pressure. As I approached my one hundred days, it became clear that I needed a new rule. Something that would remove the awkwardness from not drinking and give the people around me some reassurance that they could trust and include me in their parties.

Rule 4: Have fun. Alcohol is very well-known for giving people the confidence to do things they might never do otherwise. Such as dancing, singing, talking to large groups or anyone. Laughing, telling jokes, being silly, making memories, and being in the moment are all easier when you are on the same level as everyone else. Not drinking prevented me from getting to a point where I would wear my drunken smile all night and be the biggest participator in the group. Sober me was not this guy. It became evident that I needed to loosen up while sober. I needed to remember not to judge everyone for drinking and thus not participate. It became essential to have fun. I didn't want my sobriety to mean that I couldn't enjoy myself or that people wouldn't enjoy having me around. Having alcohol in my corner for twenty years at this point made it difficult to get past the awkwardness and the judgment I felt was hanging over me in these situations. Difficult, but not impossible. This new rule would help me through many circumstances even sooner than expected.

One hundred days. I did it. Such a relief. Now what? Time to buy a bottle of Crown Royal and celebrate? I didn't want to go back to drinking just yet. To celebrate the achievement by pouring a tall drink didn't seem like the right thing to do. *I built this moment up more than I should have, but do I just turn it back on now?* There were still so many triggers that I wanted to test myself to overcome. So many situations that I wanted to experience that weren't available in the cold wintery days of early January when I had started.

Summer was the true test for me. Could I do it? Could I go to the cottage or camping and not drink? Could I have people over to my house to swim in the pool or host barbecues and not drink? I used to make sure the cooler or

HABITS AND ROUTINES

fridge wherever I was going was as stocked as my situation at home, and others would do their version of the same. For now, I maintained I was on a break. I let the days count, and I didn't get back into drinking just yet.

"See, you did quit," friends would say.

Like the ghosts of drinking's past had converted me, and alcoholism had lost another victim. I honestly didn't feel finished with drinking. I still don't. But nobody takes this kind of break, or at least, nobody I knew had done it. That was more than a single month off.

I learned more and more about the habits and routines we develop and how hard it can be to change them. There is a lot that we don't realize. Subconsciously, we stamp these routines into our brains. Think of any habit you may have, good or bad. If you decide to stop doing this one thing, such as drinking, your brain continues to look for familiar thoughts and movements as you resume your life. If the first thing you do when you get home is going to the fridge and grab a drink, your brain, body, and "cravings" will try and make you feel like this is what you want to do.

In his book, *Atomic Habits: An Easy & Proven Way to Build Good Habits & Break Bad Ones*, James Clear says, "You need to create a new habit loop." In this example, it would be replacing grabbing an alcoholic drink when you get home with something different. Perhaps, you substitute grabbing a beer with walking the dog around the block. By doing something different and breaking the habit loop, it is easier to change the things you are used to doing and the cravings you think you have.

The other dangerous thing about our habits is that it is very easy to fall back into our old routines. That is where the cycle of twenty-one, sixty, or one hundred days is the most important. While it may take this long to create a new habit, it won't take long to fall back into an old one. If grabbing a beer when we get home is familiar, it will be easy to fall back into that routine. I didn't want to go back to my old habits just yet. I felt like I needed more time to create my new habit loop and my new lifestyle.

I was into my fourth month, and people couldn't believe I was still going. Why was there such an expectation around me to drink alcohol? Why was it so unbelievable that someone would just decide to take an indefinite period away from it? I didn't speak about it, but something whispered in the back of my mind that it would be incredible to stay away from it for an entire year. Imagine a full year away from feeling hungover and overtired from late nights of drinking. Think of the money I would save. While the money could always go somewhere else, it was never about the savings. It was about my routine, my health, and now my triggers.

A trigger is almost an overused term lately. Still, like any habit, some circumstances or actions make you feel like you need to be doing something in response or succession. For example, you reach for the cloth if you spill something on the floor. You feel cold; you grab a coat or a blanket. As I mentioned earlier, I felt the need to be drinking when I did certain things. And this was the most predominant in the warmer months. Camping, swimming, working outdoors, and engaging in outdoor activities were much better with a drink. The marketing for this stuff is targeted this way, and it is common practice for most people to want to drink during these activities. For me, this summer would be my biggest test yet.

CHAPTER 3

COTTAGE SEASON

I still hadn't told anyone I intended to see how long I could go without drinking. I was in a groove, and it was easy. My closest circle didn't push me to drink. When my friends saw me, they asked if I was still on a break, and then they would be happy for me and move on. Most spoke about their willpower and not being able to do it.

At that time in Ontario, the pandemic was giving everyone grief. Not to discount the credibility of the issue, but we lived in a smaller city with a controllable population. We maintained a low infection rate, even at our prime. With a population of around 100,000 in a large geographical area, we would often still spend time with our closest friends and family despite strict distancing rules. Restaurants and bars were limited beyond belief regarding the numbers they could have in their establishments. Things like weddings were very much on hold until they weren't.

One of my good friends had asked my wife and me to be in their wedding long before the pandemic shut things down. They had asked during a time when things were normal, predictable, and when I was drinking. We said yes, and we were still planning on being at the wedding if the conditions would open enough for my friends to have it. These are friends Ange and I have had for so long. Our wedding was one of their first dates. We spent so much time together celebrating and drinking at concerts, comedy shows, festivals, and parties; this would be so much fun.

Keeping my new goal of one year away from drinking wasn't out there yet. I was still dealing with so much anxiety about how I felt people expected me to be while out at a function. I was still very much figuring myself out. As I mentioned, I didn't know how I would handle the pressure (both internally and externally) of not drinking during moments I was used to drinking. It would be particularly challenging with people with whom I often had a drink or two while on the go. Surely, I needed to tell everyone how I felt and what I was doing. But I didn't need that pressure yet. I needed to keep doing what I was doing and take this in the smallest steps possible.

As things opened and the wedding planning was underway, the first thing was for the groomsmen to get fitted for a suit. The suit-fitting appointment was on a Sunday in the middle of the day.

"Aren't you drinking again by now?" my friend asked.

"No, not yet," I replied.

"You'd better be fucking drinking by my wedding."

The expectation and disappointment in his voice would pierce me and my anxiety about it harder than maybe it should have. Those words caused me way too much grief. They should not have bothered me as much as they did. We had spent many nights drinking together, some that we remember, some that we wished we had, and some we wished that we hadn't. It was fair for him to expect we would drink together at his wedding, but I was taking a break for my reasons. Unfortunately for the timing, the marriage now fell when I was challenging myself to change.

As long as I could stay the course, it would just be how it would be. I hadn't told anyone that I was now planning on being sober for the entire year. To be fair, this goal was constantly moving, and I really couldn't try and keep everyone around me up to date on my plan. Keeping it that I wasn't drinking *yet* was good enough for now.

"Yeah, maybe," I responded.

But in my head, I knew different. The fitting was early in the year, and the wedding wasn't until late September. I had other issues to deal with first, like how I would survive at the cottage sober.

My wife and her family had owned a cottage on a lake many years before I came along. They have a very big family who all grew up together in one cottage. They now have their own cottages and houses around the same lake with their families. They are all very close and spend so much time together. Ange and her parents had an opportunity to buy their family cottage on this same lake, one we decided to split on together.

It was an exciting time. We took possession a year before I decided to take a break from drinking, at a time when I had a routine of packing a large, heavy and full cooler for me to work on over the weekend we were there. So, it was nothing to start early with Baileys in my coffee and get into the drinks shortly after. Others were doing it as well, so it wasn't just me, but I was eager to set the pace. Whether at this cottage or any of the aunts' and uncles', I already had a comfortable cottage routine.

When we bought into this cottage, my wife and I had been together for more than ten years. Working in construction, I have never honestly had the typical vacation time many people working in offices have. My pay includes an extra percentage for the statutory holidays, and my vacation pay is paid weekly. That helps with layoff time, as it doesn't delay unemployment cheques from coming in because of vacation pay payments left owing. In a budgeting world, it would make sense for me to set any vacation monies aside and give myself a week or so off through the year. I did not do this, nor did anyone I worked with.

Because of this, if I were to take a week off during the summer, which would almost guarantee a layoff because of how busy the summer is for construction, I would have to do so with no income. When I had very young children, a wife on maternity leave, and an apprenticeship to either complete or catch up on financially, I made the most of my weekends. The cooler was packed, and because we would be committed to an entire weekend on the lake, I would easily start when we got there and drink right through the days until the night before we were to leave. After all, these were my holidays. There were problematic consistencies with my drinking way before I realized I needed a change. I am pleased that I am working on this now.

At the new cottage, the water was warm, the music was loud, and the drinks were cold. Ange has such a warm and inviting family. They spend more effort than most to ensure everyone is comfortable and has everything they need.

"Sean, what can I get you? I've got beer, rye, these vodka things, whatever you want."

"Thanks, I'll just have a water if you have one."

"Water, what's the matter? Are you hungover? Get into it last night?"

"No, thanks, I'm just taking a break," I said.

I think some knew already, but I wasn't one for the attention, and to be honest, I didn't want it to be about me and what I was doing. My wife has a couple of uncles, one of whom has difficulty taking no for an answer. It is all in good fun, and he means well, but he can be a bit of a challenge for someone who doesn't want to drink. Especially when the year before, we were both enjoying plenty of drinks while watching playoff hockey in the summer on the big screen outside his house during a pandemic-altered NHL season.

"So, you aren't drinking?" he pushed.

"Not right now," I said.

"All right, well . . . there is lots of beer in the fridge. If you want one, help yourself."

That wasn't the first time I had to stand firm and sip my water out of my security blanket mug. It continuously surprised me how unbelievable it was to people that I was taking a break. Many would continue to push drinks toward me or pry to find out more information like I was hiding some sort of unknown medical or personal issue. I was beginning to feel like this whole thing would have been easier if I genuinely did have a bigger problem. Suppose I had decided to quit altogether and attend meetings or work through programming. If there were a diagnosis, people might feel awkward and avoid the topic instead of pushing me. It felt like deciding to take a break wasn't a good enough reason to avoid alcohol for as long as I had. There must be a serious issue, not to compare my story with people dealing with more severe addictions or the victims of alcohol abuse. This is my battle, but people tend to think of worst-case scenarios when similar things happen out of the norm. By late spring, most people who'd made resolutions to stay dry for a while had found a new hobby.

I always joke with Ange that she has a fear of missing out. There aren't many functions and experiences that she misses without feeling like something amazing would happen while she wasn't there. Whether I also secretly feel the same or do not trust my friends, I will almost always be the last one standing at a function. With great pride and determination, I power drank my way through the day and night, making it to the "final battle" and outlasting everyone else. If I stayed up late enough, I might get to share a nightcap or two and a glorious ham on a bun with my father-in-law before bed. Ham on a bun was an absolute staple, a delicacy in this family, and a crown placed on a successful day at the cottage. Then, to do it all over again the next day.

COTTAGE SEASON

Working through the days at the cottage without my large cooler was a challenge at first. Any change of routine is hard, and this year, I was finding out just how many different habits I had. I packed my mug and a few things to drink. I can't stand the sugar in a can of pop, and the diet fake sugar types are even less appetizing. What could I drink if I wasn't drinking pop, beer, or fruity vodka things? The last thing I wanted to do was stand there and sip out of my water bottle, and I wanted something different. So, I brought a few bubly (flavoured sparkling water) and a couple BioSteel (a hydrating drink like Gatorade but made with fancy fake sugar). These wouldn't be too bad for me and would be a nice treat to sip on while I participated in the cottage festivities. I got creative and started mixing them as if I was making the perfect rye and Coke. Lots of ice, a splash of BioSteel, topped with bubly. I wanted to make it to the celebratory ham on a bun later.

Whether gimmicky or not, it worked. I didn't feel like I was missing anything by not drinking. And with my youngest child only about eight months old and her mother's fear of missing out, it was nice to get up early and help without feeling like death. I was able to participate, I had my beverages, I didn't feel like I was hiding anything, and I didn't feel bad. Maybe I was on to something here. I could feel a change in my routine as I survived these nights without mission drinking. I also felt less irritable, was more patient, and nicer to be around. There had been so much negativity and cynicism in me before this journey.

CHAPTER 4

CHILDHOOD LESSONS

I have a few handy friends. Whenever someone needs to cut down a tree on their property, reshingle their roof, or work on any outdoor modifications, there is no worry because help is on the way. It is an unwritten rule, though, that the fridge or cooler will be well stocked, and it is probably a good idea to fire up the barbecue at some point too. I have some great friends, but there is more pressure to drink with some than others, and there wasn't usually much in terms of alternative options. There was often a selection of ginger ale or Coke to accompany the large bottle of Crown Royal, but I don't drink pop. It was different from the cottage, where most family members knew of my intentions for not drinking, so there was minimal pressure to let myself go. This group had a different mission. One that I had been a large part of just a few months before.

As I got myself ready and left my house, I worked on my game plan. I didn't bring my security blanket this time, knowing the shit and abuse I might take if they saw me pour water from the bottle into the cup or, God forbid, drink a bubly in front of these guys.

"Are you still not drinking?"

"What is it like having a vagina?"

"Is your wife still not letting you drink?"

Ahh, guy friends. So abrasive and so direct. People had many reasons for not drinking when we were working together. Good reasons, too.

"I have to go work after."

"I have to take my kids somewhere."

"I don't want to."

I had no problem turning it down if I was busy, but this felt different. I let myself get too worried about what these guys might say or do and the kind of things I might have to listen to.

We got the job done. The guys knew I wasn't drinking, and any harsh questioning became playful jabs. Well, mostly. This group included my friend whose wedding was coming up. And there were moments where I fielded a few investigative questions about my timeline for not drinking, followed by the same statement:

"You'd better be fucking drinking by my wedding."

Deep exhale. "Yeah, we still have a few months, so I should be good to go by then."

I followed up with a quick diversion to help change the subject. I joked about my alcohol tolerance and how much of a lightweight I would be. As the days passed and the different wedding functions approached, I wondered whether six to eight months was enough time off from drinking. *Should I not drink until the wedding and then share a celebratory drink for his special day and how far I made it?* That was giving me more and more anxiety by the day. I wasn't ready to figure this out entirely yet, and I didn't want the time I spent formatting my routine to be for nothing.

I had never considered the effect before, but as I made it through the year without drinking, I enjoyed that my kids didn't always see me with a drink. What felt so innocent was probably a significant factor in how I ended up being so dependent on alcohol. I'd had a great childhood. I'd always had everything I needed and was in a safe space with my parents and two brothers.

The only thing was my parents used to be very social. My dad was a mechanic and always had people over with their vehicles for small jobs and large jobs alike. Some paid cash; some paid in baked goods. Some would bring over a handle of whiskey and spend a reasonable amount of time into the night listening to music and playing the hand drums on our kitchen furniture. One night, a friend of my dad's was passionately into a heavy drum solo on our glass kitchen table. He accidentally smashed the table with what I presumed was his wedding ring while seriously impacting the final cymbal smash of the sequence. They were quickly not allowed to play in the house anymore, and the garage man cave grew in popularity.

The nights usually started there anyways, so why not stay out there? Soon, there was a microwave, cooktop, and deep fryer on the top of the toolbox. There was a garage kitchen, and the freezer out there, while always stocked with ice, started to carry the most excellent selection of bar foods. It became normal for me and any friends who came over to pee in the modified fire extinguisher urinal that my cousin made for my dad in his welding classes. It was an impressive setup, and my parents' friends were all good people, so it was nice to have company. The neighbours started the tradition of coming over on Thursday nights and starting the weekend right. Quite often, it would be a nightly event on the weekend, but Thursday night was the kickoff. I think by now, you can understand why I feel so comfortable in the garage and why I chose it as my own safe space to reflect on this journey and write this book.

When I was young, it was never my parents' intention to cause any harm to us kids. They were very good at separating my brothers and me from the grown-up activities, but children pick up on so much. I realize this more as an adult when I see the kinds of actions and mannerisms that my kids are picking up from me. My daughter will tilt her head all the way back when she puts food in her mouth, like her dad eating peanuts or her mom eating popcorn. My sons will put their hands out to their side when they have lost something, to gesture that it was just here a minute ago. Whether you intend to or not, your kids will pick up on everything you say and do. My brothers and I sure did when we were young. Seeing my parents and many of their friends and neighbours holding drinks whenever they were over made me feel that this was the best example of how it should be. They packed a cooler to go to their baseball games, stocked up to go camping, or always maintained a stock of beverages at the house. If you asked me, I had the best training. I knew how to pour the perfect mixed drink with lots of ice and not too full that it would spill. I learned how to pack a cooler, and I knew the bottle of whiskey always went in the freezer. That is a trick that will always keep the ice colder, longer.

Aside from cleanup the next day, it was a fun game to crush all the cans, put them in a large, clear plastic bag (easier to return for the deposit) and have the next day's guests try to guess how many cans were in the bag. The game became much more fun when we had to dump the load out and get covered in old beer as we counted the cans to find out whose guess won our game. OK, only parts of this were fun, but we were helping and involved. It was the '80s and '90s, so this was tame. It set me up early for how acceptable it was to drink most days and how I should "run my business."

Before bed, it was nothing for my brothers and me to help our parents by playing bartender and mixing up the perfect rye and Coke for Dad and his friends or grabbing Mom another beer from the fridge. I can't remember how old I was, but I know I could pour an impressive drink before my tenth birthday. My younger brothers could do the same. Lots of ice, rye to the line on the cup (we used the same cups to make it easy), and top it off with Coke or Pepsi. Not too full either, as we had to carry it over to the table without spilling it. That seemed normal to me. It's where I picked up the need to stock the fridge and always be ready for a party.

As I grew, and as kids do, I paid more and more attention and learned a lot about hosting and drinking and how this is all done. I learned how it was done at home, in the garage, while camping, and even during Halloween. That was when the neighbours, conveniently spread out nicely in our subdivision, gave adults treats while filling the kids' bags with chocolate. It is amazing what kids pick up on, and I had the best teachers. It all looked like fun. Everyone who came over or was in our lives growing up seemed to have a good time, and there was always lots of booze. It was effortless to see where I got my habits. Not the drinking part, as I developed into that on my own, but the availability part. I took what I learned growing up and copied it into my life, always maintaining stock.

Around fifteen or sixteen years old, I had my first drinks as responsibly as a teenager should until I was of age (nineteen years old in Ontario). I had my share of house parties, camping trips, and events where I would drink. That was all normal and not a problem as far as I knew. But what a celebration at home when I could legally walk into the beer store, proudly show my ID, and bring these treasures home to my parents, who would not have to make the trip. My parents were very strict with me when they knew I would be having drinks. They needed to know where I would be, who with, and that I was staying the night. However, they were very understanding if I needed a ride at any point of the night and always made me feel that I could call without any trouble.

I don't think anyone was more excited that I could buy alcohol than my nana. She was a wonderful lady I miss very much, but she had her own routine that not a single person on this Earth would change. She would wake up in the morning, have her usual two cups of black coffee and then pour her first beer as soon as the coffee was gone. This beer would follow another, and another, and another until bedtime. That was also true when she smoked cigarettes. I watched her light the next one off the first one and repeat. My dad was never as bad as her for smoking. Still, I am sure that between the two of them lies the explanation for why I never touched cigarettes and can't stand being around them.

My nana didn't drive. Well, she did for a while and was safe behind the wheel, but as she got older, it wasn't worth the risk. I don't think she ever got her licence back after being stopped at a ride program one night before I was born. The officer was in the middle of the road. He had to step away from the car and tell her that she'd almost hit him. Her response was funny when we heard her tell it many years later.

"Well, I always told my kids not to play in the street."

From what I remember, one of her kids, probably my dad, had to pick her up and bring her home. My nana often called me and a few other cousins, who were also of age, to see if we would be in Trenton, near her house.

"Darling, do you mind picking me up a case of beer? I would just love a visit."

She did love the visit. Any time of day, for any reason, she loved when we would stop in and talk with her, telling our stories and where we were going in life. She was always our biggest fan. Her family was her life. I loved visiting with her and playing Yahtzee but could only stay for a short while due to the cigarette smoke.

One November morning, in college, I was T-boned going through an intersection and was in bad shape. The other vehicle was overloaded and had lost its brakes, so that they couldn't stop at the red light in time. I was taken to the hospital and then to another hospital an hour away in Kingston, where they had better equipment and services. That was at 10:00 a.m., and I know I didn't have as much as an ounce to drink the night before; I think the other driver was also OK. I do not recall that day's events or the next seven days. I remember the night before, but to this day, I lost a week where I was conscious but not very coherent and with no memory. My parents were devastated. They travelled to the hospital every day and would visit, bringing me "normal" food and testing me on my memory about the day before but with no progress. The doctors told my parents I wouldn't be home for Christmas. Finally, after the eighth day, I was coherent again.

My parents were leaving, and I said to them, "You fuckers are leaving me here, aren't you?"

They looked confused. "Hmm, yeah, you've been here for like a week."

I had no idea what had happened. So, my parents told me the story, showed me a picture of the wreck and explained what had all transpired. I had broken seven vertebrae. I had an extended cut on the back of my neck with twenty-three stitches. And I had an aggressive burn on the back of my right hand that I could only explain as road rash from my arm rubbing on the road as the vehicle did a complete spin on its side before it settled on all fours. Very lucky for someone not wearing a seatbelt.

Once I was back and aware of things, my progression was incredible. I went from being unable to walk without an attendant to walking alone without any issues. Then, quickly, the doctors sent me home. To this day, I have no back pain and no recurring problems because of this accident.

Two weeks to the day from the accident, I was home. I didn't see my nana during these two weeks as she was helping with my two younger brothers while my parents went back and forth to Kingston. When I did, I got the biggest hug I think I have ever had and the biggest shit for putting her through so much emotional trauma. She told me she went through so much more beer than usual because she was so worried about me. And for someone who would sit at her table and watch for the next visitor to come over, I can just imagine where her mind went.

In the month leading up to Christmas, I decided I would get her a Christmas gift that she (and I) would never forget. So, I framed a picture of us on the day I returned home and wrapped and put it in the bottom of a box. To fill the box, I took a two-four of beer and individually wrapped every bottle, laying them on top of this picture. I handed her the gift and watched her open it. She laughed, she cried, and she gave me another big hug.

I told her I wanted to repay her for the case that I made her drink, and through her tears, I got a usual, "Oh, you asshole!"

Through association, drinking had always been around when I was a kid and was something I came by honestly as I grew up. My father is a mechanic, and I saw many people come over with alcohol as payment for small jobs for which he wouldn't accept money. Likewise, he would refuse payment from his friends for a small job someone needed help with. Soon enough, someone added a large bottle of whiskey to his collection of liquor bottles. Over the years, I saw plenty of people pay with the same liquid currency. It was either that or baked goods, depending on who it was and their culinary skills.

It became normal for me to accept in my adult life as an electrician. For example, it was customary for me to tell someone to buy me a beer sometime as payment for a small job that I didn't need to take their money to do and then find an entire case or bottle sitting on my doorstep the next day.

That still happened as I was working through my year of change. People I had helped change lights or fix minor household issues would still drop off a bottle of whiskey when I refused to charge them for my help. They did not intend to buy me something I was avoiding; I wasn't telling people. And it was always a good gesture and one that I had encouraged in the years before. To make them feel less awkward about it, I maintained that I was only on a break, so although I couldn't share a drink with them at that moment, it wasn't a waste because I would get to it.

Maintaining the stock in my fridges or giving my grandmother a case of beer was all acceptable and expected. Growing up, my parents were responsible. We were NEVER allowed to drink anything and had a reasonable bedtime, but what harm could a little show and laugh with your kids be? I clearly learned my ways from this environment. As I continued my break from alcohol, I was enjoying my kids, not always seeing Dad with a drink. It is incredible what they pick up on.

CHAPTER 5

PASS THE ICE

As the weather got warmer, working in the yard and spending time around the pool without a drink wasn't so bad. Of course, the music was still loud, and people around me would have their drinks, but my trusty mug or even just a bottle of water or a can of bubly at this point would be OK with me. It was out there, and I didn't need to put on a show for anyone. I still had some anxieties about it, but I was improving daily. It was almost six months into my alcohol intermission, and I was feeling good. My kids and wife were seemingly happier with me too, and my routine of drinking was easily becoming a routine of not drinking.

It was now officially summer. Things were opening a bit, and people felt comfortable hosting parties and functions. Itching to participate, we didn't miss many opportunities to get out. We also had more cottage weekends, and my sober game was strong. I wasn't looking for any drinks, triggers were low, and people weren't as pushy. Ange and I had our anniversary dinner in the middle of June. We celebrated with a nice dinner and a small toast, an acknowledgement of another year together on the front lines of battle. I didn't care if people felt I should be drinking, and I felt no pressure about being in that environment.

My phone started vibrating; I never get phone calls.

"Hey, where should we go for the bachelor party?" the best man for my friend's wedding called me to ask.

Now that things were opening and the wedding was happening, it was time to plan the other wedding functions. The wedding couple wanted to do something in August for the separate bachelor and bachelorette parties, so I had another couple months to prepare my plan.

"You'd better be fucking drinking at my wedding."

Why did this matter so much? And why was it bothering me so much? It made me feel guilty like I was doing something wrong. I could understand where he was coming from, but why was it so disappointing that I was taking a break from drinking? We had some good times, and we would have good times again. For now, I tried to brush it off as passively as possible.

I wasn't prepared to sit this one out and not participate. I was sure I'd never live that down as long as we were friends.

"Remember when you stopped drinking, missed my bachelor party, and ruined my wedding, dick?"

I played out how the conversation would go in my mind. It didn't matter where we were going, I was going to be there, and I was going to get through it. The initial conversation was about a trip to Montreal or Niagara Falls. It would have been Vegas if we were able to travel. I figured I would be OK. It was only June, so there was time to figure it out.

Life was good as I alternated between sitting around the pool in my backyard and the lake at the cottage. The summer was in full swing, and I didn't feel like I was missing anything. At the cottage, my two brothers-in-law and their wives would show up with their cardboard boxes of mixed IPAs, hibiscus brews, and gin/vodka smashes in search of a spot in the apartment-sized fridge for their treasures. Unfortunately, it seemed that in a rush to get to the lake, there was no time for them to pack a cooler and buy ice.

I had my cooler-packing training thirty years ago when I was just a kid. Did everyone not get the same lessons? That was not how I was taught! Cooler, drinks, ice, and ice again for when it would melt, and repeat as necessary. Camping with my parents at a similar age was like some life lesson; if you didn't bring ice or booze, you were on your own. My dad wasn't going to babysit my cooler for me and ensure I was minded.

That was more observational than an issue. It speaks to the habits and routines I had picked up from my parents and how they would go about drinking. I did appreciate this lesson when I was drinking, as it makes perfect sense to me to be prepared when you are in the middle of nowhere.

My in-laws were fun to drink with. I always looked forward to music and time away at the cottage—even if their music was as hoppy and potent as their beer. Strangely enough, and maybe because of the music, I sacrificed being the last one awake to go to bed early. I thought, *Who and what am I becoming? I'm going to miss something amazing if I go to bed now.* Maybe it isn't just Ange that has a fear of missing out.

It was kind of funny being the sober one in the group. While I tried to follow my own rules and not be a Debbie Downer, there were moments when I questioned my drunken actions from a lifetime before. I held my own, but there were times when I was perhaps a little out of line (or a lot, depending on who you ask). There is no way I was that loud, no way I was that sloppy, and no way I was that incoherent, was there?

For the sake of our three children, my wife was completely sober for the entirety of each pregnancy and almost an entire year after while breastfeeding and anxiously caring for their every need. I don't know how she did it. She may have seen me have a beer or two too many, I can't guarantee it, but I am sure it happened. She would describe these sober moments to me and how everyone behaved. I couldn't relate at that moment, but I was now seeing this firsthand, and it was interesting.

"Hey, who wants to play Euchre?"

"I am in!"

I had been waiting for that moment all day. My kids were sleeping, and I enjoy playing cards. But this was about an hour before the famous nightcap and ham on a bun I described earlier, and this game of cards was PAINFUL! No one could remember what suit was up, whether they had discarded or who had just dealt the last hand.

The fun disappears when someone goes from the fun-loving buzz stage to the incoherent drunk stage. It becomes more annoying, and this is now going to live with me forever. Maybe this is like living my version of *A Christmas Carol*, except mine was about watching my drunken self through sober eyes and wishing I was different. Not quite the same as watching someone else, but I had a new appreciation for pacing myself once I was ready to have a drink again.

Once I was ready to have a drink again. I still thought I would only take a break for a year, but now I was overthinking my triumphant return. Should there be a celebration, a coming of age, should I invite my mom? What would my return be like? Did I even feel like drinking again yet? Would I remember everything that I learned, everything I experienced, and everything I overcame this year? So far, I was only halfway and shouldn't have been planning the celebration just yet. I still had so much to do this year. I still had so much anxiety to overcome with this bachelor party and wedding, trying to figure out how much they expected me to drink at each. For now, we had the first wedding function to worry about.

The bride and groom wanted a Jack and Jill. Also called a Buck and Doe, this is a fundraiser party put on by the wedding party to help raise money for the Mr. and Mrs. to be, traditionally to put toward the expense of their wedding. COVID still limited us on specific details, such as the hall rental, indoor capacity limits, and social distancing, but we managed to pull it off. We had an "in" with the rental and managed to sell beer at the venue to help make money for the couple (the bar wasn't allowed to serve because of virus restrictions).

There were other drinks, including a whole case of fresh, cold, delicious water. Lucky me. I was a bit beyond my security blanket mug. However, I took a certain amount of shit when I went to the best man, who was watching the bar, getting my drink of choice. While he enjoyed giving me trouble, we have a mutual shit and eat shit kind of relationship. He would help me through a few things with this wedding and the functions that would come. The bride and groom were drunk at the party and had a good time. I was proud of myself when I brushed off my friend's "you better be drinking" line this time. It still bugged me because I felt like I was letting him down, but I was sick of this expectation and the same comment about it. My six months without alcohol showed that I was serious about it.

CHAPTER 6

CELEBRATION TIME

Golf. I have had moments in my life where I have enjoyed this sport more and moments where I appreciated it less. Because I usually run hot and sweat easily, I do not enjoy myself in the hot sun, with no breeze, soaking wet, and overheating. However, I can find enjoyment in the spring and fall or on an odd overcast and breezy day. Otherwise, I would rather not bother.

I do, however, get out a few times each summer for various work or supplier tournaments, family tournaments, and now with my two boys. They enjoy it more each year as they grow, and I find new pleasure in taking them out to get some fresh air. Golf, much like billiards, darts, or for a while, anything, was much more fun the more I drank. I could easily go, have a couple, and be OK to drive, but if it was a tournament and I could help it, I would set up a ride home and be on a mission to get as drunk as possible.

Of course, I felt that I played better when I was drunk. Who knows? There could have been a sweet spot where a couple of drinks loosened me up so I would hit the ball better. But as described previously, I had a hard time stopping. I would fill my bag full of beers and never let the beer cart pass without a round.

One summer a few years ago, I had two tournaments for two different functions on the same weekend. There was one for work and one for Ange's family. It had been a long time since I went hard a few days in a row, but I succeeded with the help of a couple of spicy Caesars on the morning of day two. To be fair, I was not the only one drinking, although most didn't have the same two functions as I did and were only giving their all on one day.

I can say with confidence and shame that I have never golfed a round without having at least one drink. This year, a couple of games were coming up that I knew about. My employers held a work tournament every year that usually led to a continuation at one person's house after the game, where we would drink all night. There were parts of the night that I don't remember from last year. How had I scraped my leg? I didn't know. I hoped I hadn't been too bad.

The tournament had been booked, and I committed myself to go. It would be a lot different this year as I wasn't drinking. Another challenge I faced was the other groups of people I would be associating with. While there are similarities with the expectations to drink in each of my social circles, not everyone knew that I wasn't drinking this year. I would have to have the same conversations, answer the same questions, and reassure everyone that it was only a break.

The few times on the course this summer would tell me a different story than the one I thought I knew. As mentioned, I felt I would loosen up after a few drinks and perform better. I learned that I could achieve this regardless of drinking. That was true all along, but in my routine and with expectations set out by my age group, friends, and society, I usually golfed the same way every time. The first time I went out this year, it had been a while, so I played as expected, but in the next two or three rounds, I hit the ball better, losing less in the woods or water. Maybe confidence in sport or doing a task didn't come entirely from the booze. Perhaps I thought it did, and by having a drink, my mind told myself that I could relax, and so, in turn, I would play better. By not drinking, I could also remember what I did correctly and what I might have done wrong to make my slice so bad. I started to enjoy myself out there.

At these different tournaments, I knew how to handle myself and would easily opt out of the rounds of drinks. However, there were a few enablers, pushing everyone to get a drink and even buying drinks for people to keep the party going.

I always had a happy/sad relationship with August. It was sad because the summer was more than half over, but it was happy because my birthday is in August. Ange told me she had something booked for us to do and that I had to take the second Monday off. *The second Monday? What are you up to? Are we going away? You know that nobody will take our kids for that long.* Our parents didn't love it when we dropped the three kids off and left. They love their grandkids, arguably more than us at this point, but they didn't want them all, at once, and without us to take them home when they misbehaved. They did agree to take them for one night, though. So, we dropped them off at the cottage, prepared to take what we could get from the time off. It was nice to get away.

We went out to dinner at The Keg. Ange ordered her fancy, blended piña colada, and I thought hard about what I wanted. I wasn't ready to drink. I still had a few months left. *Heineken 0 percent, interesting. We are celebrating, and I have proven myself in ways I never thought I would. Why not? Isn't it time to test how far I have come?*

"One 0 percent, please!"

That felt awkward to say aloud. I would rather have ordered water with an umbrella in it. Zero percent beer; who even drank these, and why? If you want a beer, order a beer. The server didn't take very long, and surprisingly, the bottle didn't look like it had been sitting in the fridge for months—as if someone had left it there, and the restaurant couldn't find anyone that would take it. We hoisted our drinks, clanged them together, and took a sip. *Happy Birthday. Hmm, this isn't bad. It tastes like beer.* I only ordered the one at the restaurant, even though I felt I could have a couple more. It was clear to me why I was right not to allow myself, in the beginning, to run to these near beers. It would have been like it was for nothing, and I knew that more now than I did in January. I will contemplate the existence of these 0 percent options and their use to me soon.

CELEBRATION TIME

Ange booked a hotel within an hour of the cottage so we could be back early enough in the morning to clean up the mess that our kids must have made and head home. The hotel heard we were celebrating and had left a bottle of wine in the room for us. But Ange can't stand wine, so instead, we raised plastic wine glasses of pineapple-flavoured bubly. Cheers to another birthday. We brought the wine with us when we left, as someone would drink it, and the hotel doesn't provide those things out of the goodness of its heart. Ange didn't tell me what the night had cost, but we weren't leaving it for someone else.

A watched pot never boils. While some days went by slowly, the last eight months had flown by. I reflected on how far I had come this year with not drinking, and I was amazed at my progress. I had gotten to a point where I didn't need to drink. It was nice to get into a new routine and ignore all the subtle cues and advertising that encouraged me to want to drink before. I hadn't needed the help because I would do it regardless. It seems so innocent in the moment, doesn't it; having a drink at dinner, a glass of wine after work, a couple during the hockey game or while out with friends.

I never felt that my issue with alcohol led me to this point. It was my excessive treatment of it, how useless I would be to my wife and kids when I would sleep in after a night of drinking, and how irritable and difficult it would make me to my family, friends, and others. And I would keep going. Keep drinking after work. Keep buying and consuming an abundance of it. It was no longer about the treat and relaxing enjoyment of having a drink. It became a mission.

As the year continued, I wanted to pay attention to the situations where I would have usually been drinking uncontrollably and see how I could be happy with the person I was in that moment without drinking. Be pleased that I can put myself in that situation and not feel the pressure from others to drink; I can be there, not drinking, and still have a good time. The most challenging parts of this journey always seem to be the next parts, and I am focused. I will get through it; I am not quite sure how yet.

CHAPTER 7

THE TEST

It was one week until the bachelor party in Niagara Falls. I was still working out my game plan, how I would make the weekend successful for my buddy's bachelor party, and my personal goals. I played the different options through my head, trying to see the best ones for me to participate to the fullest. I didn't want to be the sober guy who made people feel uncomfortable or ruin my streak of not drinking. I was overthinking the whole thing. It shouldn't have been that hard for me to plan a weekend away with my friends without getting drunk like everyone else.

The group that I was going away with was some of my closest friends. Friends I have known a long time and shared many drinks and experiences with. Friends that I have grown up with and whom I loved like family. When I started this year, I was not in a very solid state, and I did whatever I could to hide my vulnerability and my choice to change. We shared the most vulnerable moments at different times in our lives, mostly while drinking, but it was still difficult to let myself stand out. The expectation for a man to be tough and never show weakness was constantly in the background with this group. I didn't yet have an experience like this while not drinking to back up my plans, but I was going to do it and hopefully not take too much trouble from the group.

If you were or weren't doing a particular thing at a specific moment, it could bring on any version of hazing and jokes. I was a participating member of this over the years, but it was not easy on this side of it, especially given the extent I had gone to this year avoiding alcohol altogether. I can't blame them for expecting I would just get over it or prove whatever I was trying to prove and move on. As I've mentioned, this was not something that anyone else had done in our circle of friends. A weekend, a week, or even a month off drinking had happened, but never a year and never at the expense of one of our weddings or celebrations. I can't blame their confusion in the matter.

Even while sober and having my full wits about me, I was still a bit uneasy letting anyone get me a drink. One, because I didn't need the extra attention of having someone throw me a bubly in front of everyone, and two, I felt like I was one playful joke away from ruining my whole year. As innocent as "accidentally" passing me a Coke or ginger ale in a red plastic cup, waiting for me to take that first sip when it's one of our usual heavy Crown Royal drinks. I wasn't going to put myself in that situation and provide everyone with entertainment at my expense. But of course,

THE TEST

I knew better. I still wouldn't be one of the first to fall asleep in front of them, either. How was I to know I wouldn't end up passed out on the rooftop, like in the movie *The Hangover*, after someone put a roofie in my shot of bubly?

To my knowledge, it was never anyone's intention to do anything to ruin my streak; it was more about "How funny would it be if we got Sean to drink?" My alcohol break hadn't been taken very seriously by this group of friends up to this point, and I felt that everyone was just waiting for me to quit being stubborn and rejoin the group. However, that wasn't going to happen, and I was about to encounter my first actual test.

We set the plans and packed the coolers. Eight of us were going, and it was going to be a great time. On the morning of the bachelor party, we all met at the groom's house and "took him hostage," not exactly a surprise, but we all played the game. Conversations leading up to our departure were consistent with any other guys' trip I had been on. We were all so proud of how much booze we were bringing, how much more we planned on buying when we got there, and that the bars better be stocked because we were on our way. We weren't much of a group for edibles, but I am sure they were also hiding in someone's bag to bring out later.

I thought about my first experience with near beer and decided to use it as a tactic this weekend. It was the easiest way to look like I was drinking and provide myself with enough of a security blanket that I would feel like I was participating and not bringing the mood down. Besides, I was able to order one at a restaurant; maybe and hopefully, this would be true if we were to go to some other restaurants and bars. In preparation, I went to the liquor store, where they sold the only 0 percent I had ever tried, and I bought a couple of six-packs for the trip. I brought my cooler, loaded with these beauties and a couple of my very masculine assortments of bubly and BioSteel that I would try and drink later while we were at the hotel and hope nobody saw. I did what I could to avoid the laughing and disgust my alcohol avoidance might bring some people.

I could have been overthinking the whole trip. The guys could have genuinely understood by now, so maybe it wasn't going to be that bad. But, on the other hand, I didn't want to wait to find out. I had to be ready and make it clear that I was there to have a good time and that I wasn't going to sit in a corner and judge everyone all night. Besides, we weren't going to be in the hotel much, and there would be way too much going on to notice me off to the side with a 0 percent beer.

I agreed to drive us to the Falls, a three-and-a-half-hour drive from where we lived. I would stay up there the day after the bachelor party and then meet my wife and kids in Toronto to continue a family version of a Toronto/Niagara vacation. I planned to load my truck with everything we would need to avoid Ange needing to bring a lot of luggage and supplies. This way, she would only bring a day bag with the three kids on the train, and we would stop at a grocery store later for a few supplies. That was way too much to fit into a weekend, we both knew it, but it seemed like an excellent opportunity to take advantage of the fact that I would already be up there.

THE TEST

If I was drinking, I could not imagine doing the family day after a bachelor party. I also couldn't imagine being on the train with three small children. So, we booked a few things for us to do with the kids. It would be strange going from bachelor party mode to family mode within twenty-four hours. So, I drove one of the vehicles. One buddy came with me to keep me company and to avoid sitting in the back of another buddy's small Ford Ranger, which was the plan for his return home the following day. It was maybe a bit nicer for both of us as there was no expectation or pressure to get started drinking any earlier than our arrival at the Falls.

There were restaurants, casinos, and bars all over Niagara Falls, and we had good intentions to see how many we could visit and how wild this night could get. We had our sights set on as many stops as we could fit in, mainly because the pandemic had shut things down for so long, and we felt we had missed out on so much. And the groom-to-be had a ten-pound bowling ball attached—excuse me, chained and locked—around his ankle, and we expected him to drag this around all night. After all, that's what he would get in a month when he was married, wasn't it? So, when we all arrived at the hotel and checked in, we gathered in one room to start a pre-drink and devise a plan.

I popped the top off one of my Heineken 0 percent bottles and joined the group. It looked like a normal Heineken and gave me the feeling I was holding and drinking a version of the same thing as the next guy. I blended in, at least until the groom-to-be's eyes lit up at the sight of my green bottle.

"Are you drinking?" he said with a smile.

With purpose, I held the bottle a certain way and covered the "0%" label with my hand so that nobody could see it. Rightfully so, companies were proud of their non-alcoholic options, but I wasn't as excited about the advertising as they were. I uncovered the label so he could see it and said I wasn't. I felt his reaction. Ultimately, I was expecting it, but the exhale and eye roll at my efforts to fit in and contribute didn't feel the greatest.

His words had almost haunted me to this point. The anxiety he had unknowingly been giving me about the requirement for me to drink at his wedding was still there. I brushed it off in the moment; honestly, I was not feeling that bad about it now. It wasn't the first time, and it wasn't a secret that I wasn't drinking. I didn't buy near beers for anyone else, although I would hand them out if people wanted. It was my decision, and he didn't need my not drinking to affect his night.

I had decided I would not drive everyone around even though I was not drinking. I just wanted to be one of the guys, drink my non-alcoholic beers and fit in. That wasn't going to happen if I was the chauffeur. I would pay my share of transportation costs like the next guy and leave my truck at the hotel. People joked about me driving everyone around, but it ended there, thankfully.

Besides getting there early and making our friend tour with his bowling ball, we didn't have much planned. So, we figured it would be a good start if we went to Hooters for lunch. After a couple of drinks at the hotel, we got ready and walked down the street for drinks and their

THE TEST

world-famous wings. I learned that while most bars seem to have at least one non-alcoholic beer option, they are not all the same, and not all are on the menu. So, there isn't an expectation that they will carry your drink of preference the same way they would if it was one of the big beer companies.

My plan to sit off to the side of the group in the beginning and see how this would play out didn't work well in my favour when I ended up seated right next to the groom. *Great, not only am I trying to blend in, but now I will try and do it with everyone watching the groom (and me!).* I was last to order a drink, panicked and ordered a Diet Pepsi. I, who doesn't drink pop and wants to fit in, order a diet pop after everyone ordered their double whiskeys, Tequila Slammers, and giant draft beers. I was not off to a good start. The worst part, and probably because she didn't care, was that the server didn't even remember to bring my drink, and I didn't want to talk over everyone at the table to get her attention to bring it.

After a few times back and forth to the table, my buddy, the groom, made sure she knew she had forgotten me. My tall glass of non-alcoholic, fake sugar arrived in a couple of minutes. He didn't do it to point out to everyone that I wasn't drinking. That was genuine, and I appreciated it.

Quickly, I finished with my soda and mustered enough courage to ask the lovely server what they had for 0 percent options. Asking the simple question of a non-alcoholic option was terrifying for me. I spoke to the server across my eight buddies, probably loud enough for the restaurant to hear me asking about their emasculating drink menu.

But, of course, she didn't know what they had and would have to check. (I would see a common theme here as we moved on with our tour, as this would happen to me often.) They stocked Budweiser Zero, and I would have a couple of those while everyone would throw back their sweet nectar.

Before any shots started flying around, one buddy came from across the table to ask me to the side if I was interested in doing shots. He knew I wasn't drinking but didn't want to put me on the spot either way. I thanked him but said no thanks. As the shots came around, I decided that if I poured my Bud Zero into a glass, short of the cans being obvious, it looked like a beer. Then, I could salute with my beer to their shots and fit in nicely.

Many of the stops on this night of celebration were much of the same. Each bar on the crawl had its version of a 0 percent that I could order. It was just as awkward each place we went.

"Umm . . ." *(Inconveniently)*, "I think we do. I will have to check and let you know," the servers would tell me.

They *always* had to check what they had for 0 percent options. At first, I was anxious about it, but it became funny. I didn't do it to mess with them; it was just what I wanted.

A few friends ordered Caesars at one of our stops, and it dawned on me that I could order other non-alcoholic options. It didn't have to be these awful near beers. I found out quickly why I hadn't thought about it, though. Restaurants and bars will serve a Caesar without vodka or any other mixed cocktail, but you must order it out loud, and they need to hear you. On a Saturday night on the town, it can be quite loud in these places, and after the first time not hearing me, the second time, all my friends knew that I wanted a "Virgin Caesar." Virgin. No alcohol. Deep exhale. The damage was done. Well, almost. I can't remember exactly, but it must have come to the table with crayons and a colouring mat.

My group of friends were nowhere close to the millennial hipster types that seemed to be a popular trend everywhere we went. A few couldn't even spell IPA. Somehow, someone, most likely the best man, decided a microbrewery would be a great idea for us for dinner. A couple of the guys were skeptical, but we knew they would have beer, and some thought they would still carry the domestic options. I knew better because of my experience at my family cottage. The food was good, and the beer seemed like it was good too. Some guys were happy with their choices, while some hated it because they thought it was too crafty and missed their domestic light beers. What non-alcoholic options do you order at a craft brewery? The only non-alcoholic option that wasn't pop or juice was kombucha. I had no idea what this was. *Brewed tea beverage, OK . . . one, please.* This pink brew showed up in its shaped glass, nothing like the beer glasses the others had.

One guy had a beer of similar colour and called across the table, "The Blanc is good, eh?"

"Hmm, this isn't a Blanc; it's a kombucha."

Belly laughing from most at the table.

"What the fuck is a kombucha?"

I still wasn't sure. It was OK, but what a ride this trip had been already. I couldn't help but laugh at this point.

From anxiety to awkwardness, each stop on tour was manageable, and I made it through. Nowhere in the night did I feel like I had to drink. I didn't miss taking shots at the restaurants and bars, I didn't miss feeling awful as the night went on, and I would surely not miss the hangover the next day. After our last bar, we trekked back to the hotel and watched the groom-to-be walk his bowling ball into his room. We had let him take it off for the last two stops, but he still had to carry it home. What a bunch of assholes we are. It was all in good fun; we all survived and made it back. I am pretty sure the best man got food poisoning from a bad chicken sandwich at the microbrewery, but he was OK. He often went to bed early when we went out drinking anyways, so when he shut it down early, we weren't surprised.

I made it through the night. I didn't feel like I missed anything, I didn't feel terrible, and I was proud of myself for showing up and having a good time. It could have been so much easier for me to stay home and avoid the temptation to drink, but that wasn't what I wanted to achieve. I wanted this experience to set me up for success. I wanted to be able to do things like this and not feel pressured to drink. For this situation, I look back and acknowledge that it was probably easier for me to avoid alcohol entirely than coasting all night. The pressure to participate in celebratory shots or to keep pace with my friends would have been a lot more if I drank a little instead of not at all. That would be something to work on next year if I drank again in the future.

For now, we had all checked out of the hotel and were on our way. I headed toward Toronto to pick up my family, and the guys headed back home. Before committing to the highway, I waited in the drive-through for a coffee, and I thought about how much I appreciated my group of friends, how supportive they were, and how easy the day before had been, even if they had given me a hard time. The whole situation I played in my head about my expectations to drink and how disappointed these guys would be at my sobriety level didn't play out how I had thought it would. Nobody had made me feel like I didn't belong. I took my share of jokes and razzing, but I also gave it back. It had been a great time. I have never been the kind of person to send what could come across as sappy or vulnerable messages, but I truly appreciated the support I had received the night before. I took the time to send our group chat a sincere thank you.

Thank you for supporting me and helping me through my decision to change this year. I truly appreciate it, and I love you all.

CHAPTER 8

TURNING THE CORNER

My large group of friends always has a big end-of-summer pig roast. The last weekend of August is a culmination of the entire summer's events and a big send-off. It is usually still sunny and hot, so it is a whole day event. We cook the pig on our homemade spit, and as it is over an open bed of coals, we start cooking early in the morning to ensure it will be finished on time for dinner. Usually, this day includes a 9:00 a.m. start where we set everything up, get the coals nice and hot, and start spinning the rotisserie.

"Everything is running; now what?"

"Dinner is at six or 6:30 p.m. Anyone for a game of bocce ball, horseshoes, or washer toss?"

"Let the day drinking begin."

Some people would not arrive until later in the afternoon, closer to dinner, but then there was the rest of us who would open our first beer before the pig made its first full rotation. That was often four to six guys out of about eighteen who would get started early. The others and our wives and children would all join intermittently throughout the day. This long day of drinking, games, music, and food was something I looked forward to all summer and something that always promised to be a good time.

In the past, I hadn't set my drinking pace very well. I would start slowly and just have a couple. But then I'd forget about watching myself, so I'd maintain a dangerous intake speed from early in the day until after dinner. Another dangerous element: I learned long ago that I do not mix alcohol well (Who does, really?). The worst thing I could do to myself was to venture very far from beer. I could maintain a steady pace of beer for the day, but as whiskey was the drink of choice for most in this group, there was always an abundance of it. There were also always plenty of red SOLO cups and someone handing mixed drinks to anyone who would take one. Never shying away from being a macho drinking type who would easily take a shot of tequila without a chaser and not even squint, I didn't let too many whiskeys pass me by. Especially if I ran out of the beer I brought and wasn't ready to stop drinking. Sober me, trying to control how much I would drink during the day, was no match for the abundance generously handed out by my friends.

Each function that passed left me with less and less anxiety about not drinking, and maintaining the status quo became easier. It helped that most of these functions were with the same group. It didn't help that the bride- and groom-to-be were also in this group. Neither did the constant questions about my sobriety and expectations for their wedding continuously lingering over me like a cloud. I didn't let it get to me in each moment, but the wedding would come up quickly, and I still didn't think they believed I would still not be drinking next month. As hard as it was, not drinking for the bachelor party was not the same as not drinking for the wedding. I was less and less worried about what people felt about my decision, but I was still a bit anxious and concerned about what my buddy would think and say when I didn't share a drink with him on his wedding day.

Ange and I stayed late, enjoying the pig roast and helping to clean up, and then I drove home. I had never been able to do that in the many years prior, as I had been a sloppy mess. However, this straight year felt good. It was a triumph that I could still have the kind of day I looked forward to and not power drink the way I used to. One thing that helped change my routine this year was this potluck event. We had all split on the pig and then brought small side dishes, salads, and desserts to compliment the feast.

We signed up for a potato casserole dish that my wife makes. It is something we often bring to our Christmas potluck and is quite popular. Due to the size and substance of the dish, it required us to start cooking it at home, and we would have to delay getting there to the afternoon so that the dish could be hot and ready for dinnertime. The potato dish was a lot for Ange to bring on her own, with our three kids and everything else, so I would have to join the event later than usual. When we arrived, a few were there for quite a while, and it was interesting to see what I usually looked like at this point in the day. There was no judgment from me as they looked like they were having a good time, and I can only speak to what I felt and what my drinking was doing to me in moments like this.

It was indeed a tremendous end-of-summer party. We had laughs and good times. Deciding to change small things like what side to bring and not being the first one there helped me avoid the power drinking routine. Next year, I may go early to help set things up and then go home to return with my family later in the afternoon. I didn't feel like I had to be there all day and be the last one up.

Within a couple of weeks, it was my wife's turn to go away for the bachelorette party. I would be home with our kids and look forward to her stories when she got home. The girls had a different itinerary than we did and would not have as far to drive. Other couples in our circle had younger kids, similar in ages to ours, and they were left behind as the girls went away. I guess I figured we would all do our own thing, and there wouldn't be a party. But soon after the girls left, I got a message that the guys would be having a BBQ. *Bring your cooler and bring your kids.*

At first, as I usually do, I told myself I wasn't going. I was not going because I didn't want to pack the kids up, bring all our stuff, and listen to everyone give me shit for staying sober while I watched them all drink. I thought about it and realized I started this year wanting to make changes, and these changes weren't going to happen while I sat on my couch. So I quickly sent a message that I was coming. I had a sleeve of burgers in the freezer that I had brought, and on my way over, I stopped at the convenience store to grab a few things. I can see this store from my house, and a couple of years ago, they were approved to be a liquor and beer distributor. Last summer, for fun, I decided to walk there and grab some beer, just to say that I had done it. It took me seven minutes. In fifteen minutes, I could walk to the store and be back with alcohol. That may have been why it was so easy for me to maintain stock and continue with my routine before this year.

I stopped at the store to grab some chips and a couple of sparkling waters to tide me over for the couple of hours I would be there. I walked the liquor aisle on my way to the fridges. I always liked seeing what new drinks were out and their glorious new combinations. I worked at a liquor store in college (over Christmas and in the summer), so I was familiar with what kinds of seasonal drinks they released. Nothing caught my eye, but I did decide it would be a nice gesture to bring over a bottle of whiskey for my friends.

After I paid, I headed toward my friend's house. This house belonged to the groom, where the wedding would be held next month. I thought it would be nice to contribute to the event with an alcoholic peace offering if you will. I am always good at buying my round, which is why I decided to purchase this bottle. How much could the guys bother me about not drinking if they were drinking my rye? It was the drink of choice in this group and went over very well. There were more jokes about them drinking my bottle without me than about me not drinking. It worked in my favour and was entertaining. My ten-month-old daughter couldn't sit still and would keep me busy, walking around the yard while the other kids played. I wouldn't have been able to drink and converse much even if I wanted to, and that was OK. After dinner, I packed the kids up and headed home. It was a great afternoon, and I was happy I had gone. I need to stop letting myself avoid functions and be more open.

The girls were at the bar. Ange texted me a few times to tell me they were having a good time. That made me happy as she doesn't get out enough as Ange doesn't allow herself many opportunities to let loose with other adults. She is always a mom.

By 8:00 p.m., after the kids were all sleeping, I watched TV and felt thirsty. I'd had beer in the fridge at home this whole time. It was one of my considerations that I wouldn't just throw it all out; I would keep it and offer it to people if they were over, or if it went bad, I would throw it out later. *Throw it out if it went bad.* Yes, you read that right. That was never a problem that I thought I would have. Beer never had an opportunity to go bad. I didn't want this year to happen without testing myself by having every opportunity to drink yet maintaining the control and willpower not to. I went to the fridge in the kitchen and looked for a snack. Then I went to the refrigerator in the garage and looked at what options there were to drink. My wife wasn't home, the kids were asleep, and it had been almost nine months. Who would know?

You can have a beer. You would get rid of the can before Ange gets home. You look after the garbage anyways. Who knows what I might have done if this had been January or February? But I was in this for the long haul. I was not going to let this ruin my challenge. I reminded myself that I wasn't doing this for anyone but myself, and if I had that one beer or more, I would be letting myself down and lying to everyone. I have more control than that, and I chose something else. Another ounce of proof that I had changed and didn't need to drink.

Sitting and watching a movie with a cold can of soda water was like when I would sit and sip on a beer. Most of the routine I was looking to change was a series of habits I had developed. A series of patterns that most people develop. In this instance, being home on a Saturday night, not having to work the next day and not having anywhere to be, and with the kids, all sleeping, cracking open a beer or pouring a glass of wine was all too typical. I almost expected it. It is precisely the atmosphere created by advertising and society, yet I felt just fine sipping on a bubly. Indeed, it wasn't the same in my subconscious, but my mindset was different. Changing something small in a big picture habit is the first step toward change. Soon, we lose the mechanism of the carbonated beverage to water or something else, and soon enough, if I want a beer, it will only be one and not all of them because I will be in control.

When Ange got home the next day, talking to her about her time away and the BBQ I had with the kids was exciting. She was always excited to hear that I was maintaining my alcohol break and how I would handle myself in different situations. She is my biggest fan, and while I am doing this year as a personal challenge, I didn't want to let her down. I didn't need to encourage her to get wasted while she was away; she wasn't the drinker she had once been, and that was OK. Who was I to judge? However, because she is always in mom mode, I enjoyed hearing that she could have a couple of days of relaxing without worrying about where the kids were and if they might need anything. Just because I used to mission drink whenever I had the opportunity didn't mean she had to.

In the past, I had been a little disappointed that my wife wasn't as much of a drinker anymore. We used to go to concerts frequently and would always share a drink or two while enjoying the show, or even more drinks if we had booked a hotel for the night. She had moved on from power drinking during the start of our young family, while I had not, and I think I had been still hopeful that she would return. However, that person hadn't returned, and while I thought it was a version of her I missed, it wasn't. She had never left. I had just been too focused on returning to that buzzed, fun state and surpassing it, so I hadn't taken a second to appreciate the glowing smile I remembered. I am unsure what I was holding on to, as we could still share a drink or two together and have a great time.

All the while I had been hoping she would come back and get drunk with me like we used to, I realized it was me who needed to change and that the drunk happy place that I longed for with her was a place that I ran past on my way to the bottom of the cooler. It's not that she wasn't the person I wanted to be with when I was drinking; I wasn't the person she wanted to be with while I was racing to the bottom. I had made it difficult for her to have a good time as I showed the same symptoms, slurring my words, being mouthy and sloppy, hiccupping and sweating, etc. None of this is attractive, yet I had let myself become this again and again. Why had I been so OK with putting this show on every time I drank? It really helped me to take a break to realize this because now that I wasn't entirely wasted and useless, I could clearly see what the end of the night looked like. I still had a few months to go, but there was a lot that I liked about myself now, a lot that I had come to appreciate without alcohol, even though I once thought I needed alcohol to enjoy these things.

September is often a slow month with school starting again, busy summer schedules wrapping up, and the weather getting cooler. I had a golf tournament for work that was a couple of hours away. I thought it would be a good way to network with our Toronto team, most of whom I had only ever met over Zoom or Microsoft Teams, with COVID being what it was. So, a few of us decided to go, and we took one vehicle from Kingston to Woodbridge. I offered to drive because why not? I knew I would be sober, and it would give the others a chance to have a couple of drinks and not worry about how to get back after the whole thing was over.

I didn't feel any awkwardness about not drinking, and most places had a 0 percent option that I could sip on at least while the others drank. Finally, we arrived and signed in.

"Here you go, guys, a bag of goodies, a voucher for lunch, and a couple of drink tickets for yourselves. Thanks for your hard work this year."

Our foursome headed into the bar to cash in our tickets.

"Sorry, sir, we don't have anything 0 percent. We only have what you see."

There was an impressive selection of alcoholic craft and regular beers, vodka fruit things, Caesars, and a line of spirits for anything you might desire.

"And we have water and Gatorade."

I don't mind Gatorade, but as everyone else was cashing in their drink tickets for tall, frosty canned beers, I was paying for my bright blue, tall Gatorade (because, for some reason, Gatorade wasn't included in the drink tickets). So, like a child, I carried my bright blue Gatorade to the cart, and thankfully, the manufacturer designed these bottles with a giant orange nipple on the top to make it easier for me to sip on, making a squeak with every drink. Whatever, it was fun to laugh at my own expense with the other guys as we played our game. Of course, they didn't have too much to say since they got to use my drink tickets for another round at the first opportunity.

While a couple of the others had my mission drinking perfected in their way, it was both fun and frustrating at points. I used to think the only way to golf was to do so while drinking a lot. I had learned earlier this year that I enjoyed it regardless, and the cool September golf course was my happy place for the sport. The others in my group were accomplished golfers, and we all took turns sharing a good shot in the best ball tournament. We were a good mix. We even maintained a respectable score until the thirteenth or fourteenth hole. Two of our team members had a great time and couldn't pull their weight on the course anymore. We didn't have as strong of a finish as we had started. It was all for fun, so it was OK. I don't ever assume I will place in any contention at these things; it was just interesting to see what I would have looked like if I were in my regular shoes. Strange that I continuously see myself in others, and I don't miss being this drunk. I don't miss it at all. I genuinely feel transformed this year. I would have never been able to see what I was like if I hadn't committed to this break.

After some mingling, visiting, talking shop, and the two guys throwing back as many drinks as they could before our two-and-a-half-hour drive home, we were on our way. With a long drive ahead, the best-case scenario was that the two would have a little nap on the way home in the back seat. One eventually fell asleep, but the other had all the world's problems solved and wanted to ensure the two of us in the front heard everything he had to say. He was talking about everything from the business's financials and how to avoid being in the red to how a team of many could partner together and make six-figure salaries with minimal worry. It was humorous and very much a seat I usually filled. I was usually the guy with all the solutions, and there was no way I was going to nap when I was in that chair. A little over halfway back, they were both awake and needed another bathroom break. Like a proper designated driver, I was hounded for the last half hour minimum by most of the others to stop at another bar on the way home, a bar we frequented during some work on the road years before.

"Come on. It's a good bar, and we need to stop anyways. Only for one beer."

I suddenly remembered why I hadn't wanted to be the driver on previous tours and had rather pay my share of the cab fee than drive. *Fine, kids . . . we will go for one hour, and then we will go.* It was nice to break up the drive, but after an hour and a half at the new bar, we were on our way. Strange that this event was on a Tuesday. I think the ones booking the event assumed we would all behave and ensure we were at work on time the following day. However, due to the long drive back and the multiple stops along the way, it was late when we arrived back in Kingston, and I was not surprised when we didn't see those two at work first thing in the morning. It was not until early afternoon that we heard from them. I knew they'd had a good time, and I was sure it was worth it, but I did not miss the hangovers and feeling like those two must have that day. They looked rough!

CHAPTER 9

THE WEDDING

The expectations and requirements of me on this day had run through my head so many times this year. I truly don't think anyone ever intended to cause me any harm, and if I had been strong enough to speak privately and confidently to my friend about what these words had meant to me, I think it would have been very different. But I hadn't wanted any extra attention, and I hadn't been that open to people about what I was trying to achieve. The pressure and expectations to be a certain way in a specific moment and my noticeable deflection had left me a bit shy and reserved about it.

To respond by saying that I was taking a bit of a break, that I hadn't quit, and "Yeah, maybe I will be drinking by then" was probably the easiest response, but it wasn't entirely fair to the people around me. These people had just been good hosts and included me in what was happening, as others had done. How often do you hear that someone is taking a break from drinking? Either you are or aren't drinking, for the most part. Entire abstinence was just absurd and unfamiliar. Reflecting on my growth throughout this year, I did the best I could with what information I had. I know I would handle myself differently today, but that is true with everything we learn and experience.

I had run into a few members of the wedding party that week, including the groom, and there still seemed to be the expectation that I would drink. While I was open and honest to people when asked, not everyone knew that I wasn't drinking. I didn't advertise it to everyone like a blatant display of heroism because I had maintained myself alcohol-free over the last nine months. Having been in a few other weddings before this point and being married myself, I knew how much of a party weddings were, especially for the wedding party. It was to be a day of celebration, and this couple deserved the best day as much as anyone else. I didn't want my alcohol break to take away from their day. But how would I blend in and pretend with every toast, cheer, shot, and salute that would come on this day? It was going to be impossible. I come from a family built on tradition, and I took pride in buying my rounds, participating in shots, and toasting with everyone at the table. I needed to ensure I had something I could toast with.

Leading up to the day, I had more conversations with the best man and expressed my concerns. Almost as laid-back as they come, he told me that it was fine and that I shouldn't worry about it. We both knew this day wasn't about me.

THE WEDDING

With an aged country landscape, an old refurbished barn, and a caterer with almost perfect reviews (booked and paid for ahead of time), it was practically catastrophic that they had to cancel it in the months leading up to what was supposed to be their special day. COVID-19 had changed so much about what they had initially planned, but it was finally here, as restrictions had opened enough that they could safely have their special day. Due to things way outside of everyone's control, and as an extra bit of insurance, the wedding was now to take place at the couple's home, in the field behind their house. They had worked extremely hard to put it all together, and it was perfect. The night before, the wedding party met to help set up, run through the rehearsal, and have one final visit before the event.

Because it was at their house and there was no liquor license, it was a BYOB event, which worked for me as I could plan my own 0 percent and sparkling water options without worrying. I already had the most successful New Year's resolution this year, but I still wasn't sure they knew I wasn't drinking at their wedding. I think they felt I would be back and only needed a break to this point. I have always lacked self-control when it comes to the all-you-can-eat buffets, thinking that I need to get my money's worth or ensure I try as much as possible to maximize value. That isn't healthy and is something that I need to work through. The same can be said about an open bar. To have no financial limitations on how frequently we consume drinks is a recipe for disaster. While my old self would have wheeled in the largest, fullest cooler for a wedding such as this, I was thankful this wasn't an open bar. I had the means to avoid drinking, but the further temptation would have made things increasingly difficult.

My friend was disappointed that I wouldn't be drinking, and the reality of my decision was setting in. As part of their wedding favours, they bought a different bottle of alcohol for each of the twenty tables to use as a 'shooter' and gave everyone engraved shot glasses with the date of their special day. Everyone in their wedding party also received a special engraved insulated drinking cup. There was a moment while we were getting ready when all the groomsmen toasted in the driveway. I toasted with water. That was already way harder on me than I had thought.

Most likely because of a conversation we'd had just the day before, I noticed the best man was talking to the groom about my not drinking and defending my choices. Most were OK with it by now, and though I took some more chirping, even the groom came around. His disappointment was evident as they shared a toast of Drambuie (which the three of us had done many times together in years before), and I heard a few more jabs about my choices. I appreciated his disappointment when I didn't participate fully in the toasts at the head table with the provided drinks. But this wouldn't be the defining moment in their wedding. My decision not to drink didn't stop me from being there or having a good time, and it didn't take away from their day and evening together as new husband and wife. My anxiety leading up to this day was almost entirely in my head as I felt I was letting him down. But to be fair, his comments and continuous "threats" that "I had better be fucking drinking at his wedding" were so much harder on me than he must have realized.

It was a great night. My drinking didn't matter to the outcome, although I had to spend considerable effort dodging various shots and some homemade Jell-O shooters through the night. As I poured my 0 percent beer into my new engraved, insulated mug during the wedding speeches and toasts, I thought, why are we so worried about what others are consuming or whether they have coffee, water, beer, or syrup in their glass at any given moment? Even with a 0 percent alcohol beer that tastes similar, why do other people care so much? The mechanism is still there. The gesture of my toast or salutation isn't any less meaningful because of the alcohol content of my beverage. I did not waste the insulated glass because I had water in it. The expectation to drink alcohol and the symbolism people associate with it is very hard to change, even if it is only myself that I want to change. I didn't ask anyone else to change their routine, and I didn't need anyone to feel a certain way because of what I was doing, and yet, naturally, people did.

I have always been more aware of my surroundings than most, and I am naturally a people watcher. In a similar fashion to other events this year, I picked up on a few things other guests had been doing while under the influence. I feel like I will have alcohol again, but I like being in control, not making myself feel sick for the next day after a function, and remembering entire events rather than blacking out. When this year is over, I will have to decide my next move and how I want to proceed.

Ange and I returned to the house the next day with our kids to help clean up. Everyone was mobile, and we reflected on how much fun we'd had the night before. There were a few comments about how I must be feeling, having not drank the night before, but overall, it was a positive moment. I believed I had now just passed the most significant hurdle this year.

The feeling that I had built up for this wedding and how I felt others around me had perceived my decisions reminded me how easy it is to get ourselves worked up. So even though there may have been legitimate disappointment that I wouldn't be drunk at this wedding, I am sure it wasn't as bad as I made it all appear.

I was working on being different this year, and even though I found so many resources and conversations that had helped me through, there just wasn't much content that spoke to me and the journey I was on. So how does someone decide to take a break from drinking and manage their previous relationships, carry themselves in similar moments, and essentially teach themselves to have fun without something they have been so accustomed to having in their system?

Arguably, before I started drinking at these types of events, I was just a child. *If* I was allowed to come to an event such as a wedding, I was there with my parents, possibly only for a part of the night and very likely at my own miniature table with the other children. Before this year, I didn't have a benchmark for how this would play out. The lack of alcohol and my security blanket heightened my anxiety about "my performance" at the event. Would

I be funny enough? Would I be sincere enough? Would I still fit in with my friends? Would I look like I should be seated with the most influential people in the new couple's lives? And would I look like I wanted to be there? I hadn't wanted to be anywhere else. I had been genuinely excited for this day and everything it had brought. It had been a decade in the making.

As much as this was the most significant function I had to prepare for and overcome, everything I did this year taught me more and more about myself and what I was capable of.

CHAPTER 10

NO UMBRELLAS

Following the wedding, there were a series of small events I didn't have any issues dealing with. Being alcohol-free was not as difficult now because my anxiety about what people thought was almost gone, so I didn't need anyone's approval. My "rules" were still critical to me, and so was how my inclusion in certain events appeared to others, but it was more a courtesy to them than a necessity for me at this point. To "look the part" or to facilitate the appearance of holding a glass/drink as I conversed with a person across from me who was doing the same conveyed the body language that we were the same. There was no feeling that I was any different, nor did I judge those who continued to have alcohol.

Being ten and then eleven months alcohol-free and around some of the same people, it still surprised them that I had remained committed to the year.

Surely you have proven your point and can have a drink now, many friends would say.

Indeed, I was craving a beer and the Irish cream in my coffee on the weekends that I used to love, but I was going to make it to my goal, and I would decide how to satisfy my cravings then.

As some functions came and passed and more extended family found out about my goals, people were very proud and happy for me. I appreciated all the positive attention, but I also needed not to let myself get caught up in it. I had been in a darker place when I started the year, and I needed to remember the beginning as I neared "the end." If I allowed myself to forget what had led me to this point, why this was important, and why I still needed the last two months, it might have all been for naught. Taking this extended break, during which I learned how to handle myself, take part without alcohol, and remember my triggers, was going to be the only way that I fixed my old routine. More than anything, if I didn't make it to the whole year, it would feel like I had failed, making it easier to pick up where I had left off before this had all started.

With a hectic summer at work, a few of us decided to plan a weekend away. Some time at the casino, perhaps some golf or go-carts, and some well-deserved rest and relaxation were in order. With minimal COVID restrictions but options still somewhat limited for travel beyond Canada, we decided Niagara Falls was a good plan. We split on the hotels and picked a date. Early November was a good time to go. It wasn't too cold, and enough was still open to fill the days. I had done a version of this trip already; I knew my game plan, and I wasn't worried. We all drove together, and the conversation about my drinking came up very early on in the trip. One friend asked if I would have some drinks with them.

"You aren't going to have some drinks with the boys? Not even a shot? You've made it this far; couldn't you have a drink and then go back to not drinking?"

My short and long answer was no. I had already packed a couple of six-packs of 0 percent beer for drinking at the hotel, and I was familiar with what options were available at the casino and bars in Niagara Falls.

Having that sober guy hanging out while everyone else is drinking is always awkward. It was also brought up. There were comments about how I would remember everything, how I would participate, and how I would judge. These guys didn't know how important my "rules" were to me or that these "rules" even existed. They didn't need to. There wasn't going to be a way for me not to remember what happened, but I intended to go, have a good time, and enjoy the weekend. Once again, others around me were more worried about how I would handle myself than I was.

After arriving, checking in, and having a drink at the hotel, we headed toward The Keg for dinner. What better way to celebrate a busy season at work and a guys' weekend away than a filet mignon or prime rib meal at The Keg? (Royalties, please!) The server went around the table and took drink orders. Due to COVID-19, we were to scan the bar code and read the menu from our phones. The menu showed that they had Heineken 0 percent, which I enjoyed. The others ordered their Keg-sized draft beers, Keg-sized

Caesars, and double rye and Cokes. When it was my turn, I awkwardly ordered my 0 percent. After some attitude from the server about whether they had it or not—I was not sure where that came from—I decided to order a virgin Caesar instead.

In front of four other construction co-workers on a Friday night at The Keg, away from our wives and families, with confidence, I ordered a VIRGIN Caesar. Of course, that would have never happened if I had given myself this test at the beginning of the year, but I wasn't ready for it then as I am now. I tried to joke with the server that I would like an umbrella in it as if suggesting an umbrella would make it more flamboyant, but it was so I could tell the difference from the normal Caesars that the guys ordered.

She wasn't having it. "Sir, we don't have umbrellas."

Clearly, she couldn't read the situation. After a virgin Caesar and a couple of the Heineken 0 percent they found in the back of the cooler, we headed out to do a small bar/restaurant hop along the main strip in the Falls. We were too full to do anything too far and fast.

As we toured between bars and I took my turn ordering my alcohol-free options, others felt obligated to point out what I was doing at different times. When I ordered, they thought it was their duty to let the server know I was taking a break from drinking. It happened more than once and struck me as strange. The servers didn't know me from Adam, and why would they care that I was taking a break? What does it matter? Somehow, the guys felt it was an important detail in their state.

"Oh, he isn't an alcoholic; he just quit drinking."

Would it have been essential to point out if I was a recovering alcoholic or wasn't drinking because I had hurt myself or someone else? I doubt anyone would have brought it up, but because I was only taking a break, it was something the server should know. Adding to the awkwardness of ordering, an absolute consistency with the servers I encountered (and not only on this trip but others too) was the lack of knowledge of the 0 percent beer options. Every single time, the server had to check what they had. It guaranteed that I would be the last to get served, but whether the server knew what they had available or not, I was impressed that most places had at least one non-alcoholic beer available.

As the night went on, one thing that surprised me was that I had one server questioning why I was even at the bar. As it was after midnight and I was sipping on another 0 percent, she asked about me being out while not drinking. The others were all on their way, and I wasn't doing shots, I wasn't ordering as many drinks, and I wasn't as loud. I'd had a few 0 percent beers throughout the night, and I still took a couple of turns buying rounds for the group, but why was it such a surprise that I was out having a good time? What was her problem? What did it matter? I'd paid my cover just the same, and I wasn't hurting anyone. I didn't have a curfew. Just serve the drinks and mind your business.

Like the last guys' trip to Niagara Falls, I woke up feeling great. No headache, no stomachache, and no regrets from the night before. It is such a different feeling to get away and not come home more tired than when I left, like any and every other guys' trip I had ever been on.

I couldn't say the same for the others, though, as it was a slow start to the day. I didn't mind relaxing as the others got their wits about themselves and got moving. We left the hotel and figured we would end up somewhere to stay over the lunch hour. We found Hooters not very far from our hotel at 11:00 a.m. They were just opening, and our server was clearly in rough shape from her drinking the night before. We were the first customers at Hooters for the day, so who were we to judge?

After we ordered drinks and wings for brunch, my Bud Zero didn't hold a candle to the one guy's double tequila, Jägermeister, and Red Bull. Even during my greatest drinking moments, I wouldn't have ever ordered something as aggressive as this, especially as the bar had just opened, and this was not at an all-inclusive beach resort. He would surprise me a few more times this trip. I love the guy like a brother, and he would show me a few things I could be proud of, but it was also the drinking routine I was training myself to leave behind.

Day two was spent barhopping and going to restaurants, some time at the casino, and then more hotel drinks before we were back at the hotel with plans to be on the road early. As we made sure the one guy made it to his room, I wasn't sure what everyone else would be like in the morning. At that moment, whether the nickname they tagged me with of Sober Sean was a bad thing or not, it truly made me appreciate the division between being completely wasted and sloppy to being sober and coherent. There is a happy medium if you can control yourself. This happy medium is where I would like to see myself in the future.

NO UMBRELLAS

Barhopping isn't as much fun when you're sober. I would feel like we had just gotten situated, and then the others would want to get going again. I learned something else on this trip that I hadn't realized yet. As the night was getting later and the music and noise were getting louder, I would get more and more uncomfortable. Trying to look like I was having a good time was more challenging. The louder and louder the environment got, and the drunker and drunker the others got, the further and further, I wanted to be from the situation. Thankfully, in our crawl, we didn't stay in too many places for very long.

I truly appreciated this trip, and everyone had a good time. On the ride back home, it was funny how rough a few of the guys felt. It was a picture that I won't forget, the pile of hungover bodies across the back seat with a three-hour drive ahead of them to hopefully not throw up all over. Thankfully, they made it and laughed at how rough they all felt. I smiled on the inside. I didn't want to brag too much. Nobody wants to be that guy standing on his pedestal, and nobody wants that guy around.

CHAPTER 11

YEAR'S END

December had arrived, and Christmas was here. The warm cream liqueurs, peppermint-flavoured delights, and the biggest and best gift packs would be released just in time. Who doesn't need a liquor bottle for Christmas shaped like a hockey skate? These gift packs are fancy, and it is so hard not to buy one for everyone on your list, including yourself. In years past, I often bought a couple extra just in case I needed a rogue gift for someone I'd forgotten. That was another trick that I learned from my dad. He would do this, and I have seen it work. Someone would come over that he wasn't expecting, and he would pull one of these out as if it was for them the whole time. And if it didn't get handed out, it was still a win—a new bottle of alcohol, complete with fancy new glasses or bar trinkets for ourselves. I looked forward to seeing what the latest gift packs would be. It was dangerous when I worked at the liquor store over the Christmas season a few times, as I had a front row seat to what was released and could buy whatever I wanted before they were all sold out (never at a discount, unfortunately). There were so many things that had a Christmas flavour or accent put on them that I usually looked forward to. Who knew you could add peppermint to so many things, and they would be much better? And who couldn't use a plethora of new glasses with their favourite drink etched into them?

By now, I was entirely out of the routine of drinking, my cravings were non-existent, and I was feeling terrific about how far I had come. My close group of friends had a Christmas party we planned to attend. It was a potluck dinner, and in years past, much like at the summer pig roast, I would find myself very drunk and not well. However, I wasn't worried about that this year, and I had a good time. The party was at the bride and groom's house from the summer, often where our parties were held. After dinner, my friend passed around a bottle of festive peppermint RumChata for people to take shots of. As he offered it to me, he remembered and then pulled it back.

"Oh yeah, it's not New Year's Eve yet."

Hmm, thanks for that, I thought. I didn't know why it had to be so awkward. Perhaps this was a leftover sentiment because I hadn't drank alcohol at his wedding. Or maybe it was playful, and I was overthinking it. If the roles were reversed, I'm sure I would have had my own things to say. Instead, we played some festive games, had some good conversations, and enjoyed being able to see each other again. I had a conversation with the bride about what I had achieved this year by not drinking, how we both felt about inevitable drama, and how she also agreed that she didn't like the expectation of drinking every weekend, all the time. This talk helped put to bed the thought that my not drinking had negatively affected their wedding.

It was interesting that it had all come back around to this situation. Sure, I didn't start the year with the comments about my not drinking, but it had been the underlying cause of anxiety for me for some time, and my friend saying, "Oh yeah, it's not New Year's Eve yet" reminded me that I was on the right path and had made the right decision.

Due to my procrastination at the beginning of the year and my reluctance to get started, New Year's Eve wasn't the last night of the year off for me. Instead, it signalled the final major milestone since I wouldn't be tempted to drink on the last few days leading up to January 4, as we would be cleaning up after Christmas, etc. Ange and I were planning on bringing our kids to spend New Year's Eve at her parents' house. I sipped on a couple of zero-percent beers throughout the night, and it would be everything the group of us could do to get to the countdown. With young kids and an overall busy year, I am surprised we made it without going to bed early. Minutes to midnight, my sister-in-law poured champagne to toast the new year. True to my mission, I passed on the champagne and had orange juice. It truly isn't the substance as much as the intentions and the meaning that matter.

Four days later, I made it. 365 days. One full year. If I'd asked myself in January 2021 if I genuinely felt that I would be able to stay away from alcohol for an entire year, I would have thought it was impossible. Thinking long-term about any goal makes us naturally cringe and ultimately fail. But, unknowingly, breaking down what ended up being my goal into increments of one month, two months, one hundred days, and then one full year helped me focus on taking the smaller steps to achieve the larger goal. In the moment, I didn't even realize that this was what I was doing. It wasn't until later in the year that I learned the significance of breaking down a goal and completing it in smaller, more attainable sections. It still would have been difficult to think I could have done it because I had never tried, and I didn't have anyone I knew to compare myself to. I have listened to many conversations and audiobooks that have confirmed that this tactic works.

Because I felt like my drinking, albeit problematic at times, wasn't a big problem, I didn't think I fit the profile for needing a coach or sponsor to keep me on track. Looking back, a coach or sponsor would have helped me so much, as I could have reached out in moments when I felt weak or confused. So many people questioned my motives, the duration of my break, and why I thought I needed one. The stress of that and all the mechanisms I tried to fit in or participate in might have been things I could have had help trying to control. Someone who had similarly been through this would have helped me stay focused when I had to be strong enough to push myself to continue. While these resources are out there, and we need to be strong enough to ask for help if we need it, perhaps, to be successful, I needed to explore myself and find my own way.

YEAR'S END

Even with COVID-19 having shut many things down at different times this year, I had a good number of experiences and opportunities to test myself and learn. With the wedding, the two guys' trips to Niagara Falls, the first summer at the cottage, and many family and friend socials over the year, I can confidently say that I didn't reach my goal by hiding in my house and avoiding everything. I needed to be still involved and present at these functions. My development over the year did become easier at each event, but I also couldn't help in certain moments to avoid going. My group of friends gather for drinks often. Some will go weekly to a local pub on Friday afternoons, house socials, dinners out, etc. I sometimes found that I would either come up with an excuse not to go or find myself seeing posts on Facebook and wondering if I wasn't invited.

I found myself now trying to decide how I would reintroduce drinking without falling back into my old routine. I decided that I wasn't quite ready, and I would take the next few weeks or so into January to process last year and make my observations while still in the same mindset.

The support I received from people around me was incredible and even more remarkable that some wouldn't let go of the fact that I wasn't drinking again yet. Even my brother, who, as mentioned earlier, was more worried about whether I had received my gold coin than how I was feeling or how things were going, would invite me out for a beer on purpose and then roll his eyes at my polite decline. Perhaps it wasn't as he intended, but it seemed like he was poking at me and didn't make me feel very good.

The conversation and the offer could have come across as less derogatory as it was not like this was new. However, as time passed, he came around and offered me plenty of support. That is an example of how difficult it can be to manage our support for people going through things that we may not completely understand.

Not drinking again immediately also allowed me to see a new round of family and friends go into their version of Dry January. It is vital to understand that we all must hold ourselves accountable and realize that we all do things differently. I wasn't watching those around me to judge their actions but simply comparing them to how I did or could have done it. A few close friends and family told me I had inspired them to give Dry January a shot. I watched some dive directly into the 0 percent beers without much of a break and at the same volume. I heard from those who are now excusing themselves as they struggled to avoid drinking, explaining how they would give it a week or two.

In January of last year, I hadn't planned on going as long as I did. However, I am happy with how I did it, and I felt good when a few asked for some pointers on how they can be successful in taking their own breaks. I learned so much this year and have been feeling great. I am less irritable, more helpful with my kids, in better shape, and have an overall better outlook on myself.

That isn't all from taking a break from drinking. It is also from changing my routine and staying focused, which allowed me to open up about other things and change some things about myself that I wasn't proud of. Deciding how to approach reintroducing myself more casually to drinking became difficult because of those around me. Not everyone knew about the thoughts and feelings that led me to start this break last year and were quick to take a deep exhale on my behalf and try to pass me a beer to celebrate when the year was over. I'm not sure that is the correct way to do it. It isn't about rushing back to it for me at this point, and I don't want to celebrate by throwing back a few. It was to make me a better person. Some were quick to try and push it on me, while others were surprised that I hadn't started on my own.

"You made it the year, so what are you waiting for?"

"See, you did quit."

So, what if I did? What does it matter to people if I don't drink? My wife and I thought it might be better that when I decide I want to, I can have a casual drink with her while we play cards or something, and then any pressure I might feel won't be there, and so I can brush off the celebration portion if my friends try and welcome me back.

At the time of publishing, it has been a year and a half since I started this journey. Once I decided to write about this experience and reflect on the journey, I decided that it would be best to maintain a clear and sober state of mind. Although, while considering returning to drinking in some form, I felt comfortable that I may not dive back into my old routines, I didn't want to work on a book about going dry and becoming sober while drinking a beer. The importance of staying sober during this writing has also led me to think that I don't want to return to the way I was. The parts I miss about drinking, and the feeling I have when I open a beer on a nice sunny day when I am working outside, while with friends or family, or in any of the other moments I was used to having it, have all passed. If I want to have something, I can still have something non-alcoholic. I still have a few regular beers in my fridge for people who come over; I don't think they are expired, but I should look into that. I keep a couple of 0 percent available if I want to have one, but I am so far away from where I was with the kind of stock I always felt I needed to maintain. I have frequented the cottage a few times and have not felt like I needed to bring the volume that I was used to, alcoholic or not. One time, I may get a small pack of near beers to sip on around the campfire; other times, I don't bring anything and drink water.

    I do not have any cravings for the person I was at the start of 2021. The journal entries, the way I wrote about my attitudes and how I felt is not a place I want to go back to. However, accepting where I can be most vulnerable, listening to the inspirational content, and reading as many books as possible have put me in such a great place mentally. I am no longer the person who feels this stuff is not for me. Like me, people who need it the most may not even know it exists yet. I am not the same person I was last year, and I feel so much closer to Ange and our kids.

    I am warm and patient with them, whereas I was always the opposite before. I am motivated to play soccer or pull the kids in the wagon on the streets around the house or cottage, and I can see the difference in my kids in how our relationship has grown. I shed a tear thinking about how difficult and lost I was before and about the kind of father my kids could have had before this year. Did everyone around me suffer because of how I was? More than my craving for a beer or a shot of Baileys, I want my kids and my wife to get the best version of me. Their quality of life and how my attitude and influence come through in their lives mean more to me. I still maintain that I am on a break.

Like anything personal that I am working on, it will be my choice whether I want to participate; it will not be the decision of another person or what some may expect of me in the moment.

CHAPTER 12

IT'S YOUR TURN, CHALLENGE YOURSELF

Whether it is a drinking routine like what I went through this past year or any other habit you want to try and change, you can't do it for anyone but yourself. You are the only one who can hold yourself accountable when it matters the most. There were a few moments this year when it would have been effortless for me to have a drink. When my wife and friends weren't watching, I could have "accidentally" slipped on the near beers when I introduced them, or I could have hidden a few shots while away from home. While this would have been easy, it wouldn't have helped me change my routine. It would have all been a lie. To stay committed, whether with my friends and family or by myself, was crucial in successfully changing my routine.

If we strive for change because others are forcing us to, it is not easy to do, and we will often fail. There have been things in my past that I was working on because someone was pushing me to change. Luckily, those things weren't dire, but regardless, I started to loathe the person. I started associating them and their attitude about what they were trying to change with only negativity, so I wasn't looking at the positive factors that might come out of it. Because I didn't want to change, I wasn't going to, so I would hide things from them, lie about my progress, and then wonder why it didn't work. Naturally, lying to others is much easier than lying to ourselves.

You can likely relate to some of the material if you have read this book. Perhaps you have things you would like to work on in your personal life. Perhaps there is a part of you that wants to be different. Whether it is to stay away from alcohol, diet, exercise more, or any other personal goal you may have, the time to act is now. Nobody is going to do it for you. Start by accepting the resources and assistance that are around you already. If the people in your life aren't very supportive and give you some trouble and negativity, so you can't be honest with them, they aren't the help you need to succeed.

I had some of my best friends give me the most challenging time. These people are still in my life, but certain people just weren't the ones I needed to help me get over the hump, just like maybe I wasn't the person in the past to help them with their lives because of where I was at with mine. So we all go through things differently and at different times. But I am confident that I have the resources to help me now more than ever, and I know you can do it too.

Thinking about anything in the big picture almost invariably causes us to fail. For example, we look at losing 100 lb as a huge step, and it *is* a huge step. To do it all at once is near impossible. But when we break it down into smaller goals and smaller sections, we can train ourselves to keep going and celebrate small wins. The end goal isn't so bad; soon, we look back and wonder how we could do it. Keeping track also helps us visualize the process, and it feels so good to add more checkmarks, circles, or whatever you want to use on the calendar to mark these small victories.

One day at a time is not just a terrible cliché; it is the truth. Mark each day you took a walk, got ten minutes of light exercise, didn't snack on junk food, brushed your teeth twice a day, didn't have any alcohol, or whatever you may want to work on because it feels so good when you see it on the calendar. My calendar was so full of marks, circles, and notches last year for the few things that were important to me to change, and I have already started this year with an excellent head start. I leave this calendar in my garage, where I get ready for work each day. It helps me by being in a very convenient place, but you may decide you don't want to risk anyone looking at it and asking questions. That will be something you will have to work out on your own. If you hide it from others, you will most likely hide it from yourself. The significance of the subtle marks versus keeping an open log (which isn't a bad idea) is that only you know why you circle days, but if you need to explain it to someone, you can tell them whatever you want. For example, "I am just counting down the days until the summer." Something that isn't significant to them and may help change the subject.

So, my challenge is to pick something that has been bothering you that you want to work on to better yourself. Mark a big circle on the calendar for the first day and for every day you do it. You will start to feel upset for missing days and hold yourself accountable. The circles will pass with each day, and you will begin to feel so much better that you can do this. Commit to doing this for one hundred days when you decide to start. It has worked so well for me. It is a good three and a half months of training yourself to make this who you are.

Make sure you celebrate this magnificent achievement when the one hundred days are up. You deserve it. I would suggest not celebrating in such a way that will jeopardize what you just worked so hard to overcome, but the celebration is essential. It rewards us for putting in the work and gives us the dopamine to want to continue. But, of course, the things we work on are of all varieties, so one hundred days may not be enough. You need to judge this for yourself.

I am not here to tell you that this is the perfect solution. Like every other piece of advice and written support, you need to make it your own. Take the key factors and fit them into your life. That is true for most material I listened to last year. I think David Goggins' story is so inspiring and so very real. I listened to his book, *Can't Hurt Me: Master Your Mind and Defy the Odds*, three times last year and will be doing so again. With my young family, work responsibilities, fire department responsibilities, and an incomparable life to this point, I couldn't make his story my own. However, I could take his drive and inspiration, transfer it to my situation, and push myself when things get hard. And I could use his influence and experience to toughen up when experiencing my discomfort and inconvenience. And in my progression, perhaps I can push myself to use more of the tactics he describes in the future. That doesn't mean I can do anything he did, but people like him push us to be better and not let our minds get the best of us.

Do this for everything you read and listen to. Decide how to make the concepts of others work best for you. I am fortunate to have an hour commute to and from work and decided to use this time to my advantage. If your life can't accommodate two hours a day of inspirational content via podcasts or audiobooks the way that mine did, don't be upset. It isn't practical for most people, and when working from home or sometimes on the weekends, it was tough to find the time to keep on it. You should be able to find the time somewhere in your life if it means making yourself stronger. When I wasn't travelling, I could take time to do this while cutting the grass, cleaning the house, or in the evening before bed. With three young kids and my other obligations, I may have never gotten the information I needed to change if I didn't have the time while driving to work to listen. Fit it into your life how you can and stay specific to the things you want to learn about the most.

Thanks so much for reading my story, and I hope you can find some strategies, information, or inspiration through my experience to try and work on a few things of your own. There is a ton of information out there, so much so that we don't have to expose ourselves to others if we feel weak. Through listening to podcasts, audiobooks, and reading books, the information can help point you in the right direction. Once you hear a few things you like, it becomes easier to try different tactics that might work for you or come up with your own. As deep and dark a place as I started this year, I finished it with a much clearer mind and purpose. I wanted to share this experience with anyone it may help, much the same as the content I listened to did for me this year. Please take my story and apply whatever fits to the area you want to change or where you are in life. You will feel so much better, and you won't regret it.

    Sean

ABOUT THE AUTHOR

Sean Robinson is thirty-seven years old, works in the construction industry and is also a volunteer firefighter. He lives with his wife and three children in Ontario, Canada. *Going Dry: My Path to Overcoming Habitual Drinking* is his first book. Learn more at www.seanrobinson.ca.

www.ingramcontent.com/pod-product-compliance
Lightning Source LLC
Chambersburg PA
CBHW050258120526
44590CB00016B/2406